Technology and Work in Services

Valeria Cirillo · Matteo Rinaldini ·
Maria Enrica Virgillito
Editors

Technology and Work in Services

Vulnerable Workers under Automation
and Digitalisation

Editors
Valeria Cirillo
Department of Political Sciences
University of Bari 'Aldo Moro'
Bari, Italy

Matteo Rinaldini
University of Modena and Reggio Emilia
Reggio Emilia, Italy

Maria Enrica Virgillito
Institute of Economics
Sant'Anna School of Advanced Studies
Pisa, Italy

ISBN 978-3-031-88148-0   ISBN 978-3-031-88149-7 (eBook)
https://doi.org/10.1007/978-3-031-88149-7

© The Editor(s) (if applicable) and The Author(s), under exclusive license to Springer Nature Switzerland AG 2025

This work is subject to copyright. All rights are solely and exclusively licensed by the Publisher, whether the whole or part of the material is concerned, specifically the rights of translation, reprinting, reuse of illustrations, recitation, broadcasting, reproduction on microfilms or in any other physical way, and transmission or information storage and retrieval, electronic adaptation, computer software, or by similar or dissimilar methodology now known or hereafter developed.
The use of general descriptive names, registered names, trademarks, service marks, etc. in this publication does not imply, even in the absence of a specific statement, that such names are exempt from the relevant protective laws and regulations and therefore free for general use.
The publisher, the authors and the editors are safe to assume that the advice and information in this book are believed to be true and accurate at the date of publication. Neither the publisher nor the authors or the editors give a warranty, expressed or implied, with respect to the material contained herein or for any errors or omissions that may have been made. The publisher remains neutral with regard to jurisdictional claims in published maps and institutional affiliations.

Cover credit: © Melisa Hasan

This Palgrave Macmillan imprint is published by the registered company Springer Nature Switzerland AG
The registered company address is: Gewerbestrasse 11, 6330 Cham, Switzerland

If disposing of this product, please recycle the paper.

To the vulnerable, *often* invisible, *workers around the world and within our everyday lives*

Acknowledgments

This book builds upon the findings of the research project "Case Studies of Automation in Services" conducted in collaboration with the Human Capital and Employment Unit of the Joint Research Centre (JRC) of the European Commission, Seville.

The contributors gratefully acknowledge the support received from the JRC Human Capital and Employment Unit team, including Enrique Fernandez Macías, Marta Fana, Annarosa Pesole, Matteo Sostero, and Cesira Urzí-Brancati, during the research activities.

The authors extend their appreciation to the HR staff, IT technicians, workers, and trade union representatives from Poste Italiane, Amazon, PMI Manufacturing and Technology Bologna, Santa Maria Nuova Hospital Reggio Emilia, Azienda Sanitaria Unica Regionale Marche, Humanitas Research Hospital, Coopservice, Nestlé Vera, and Dussmann Service Italy for sharing insights about their work practices. Special thanks are due to Poste Italiane, Amazon, PMI Manufacturing and Technology Bologna, Santa Maria Nuova Hospital Reggio Emilia, Azienda Sanitaria Unica Regionale Marche, Coopservice, and Dussmann Service Italy for accommodating in-person visits to their establishments.

The completion of this book was made possible through support from the Italian Ministry of University and Research under the PRIN2022 project (2022Z78M8J): *The Digital Transition and the World of Work:*

Labour Markets, Organizations, Job Quality, and Industrial Relations (DIGITWORK).

The editors would also like to thank Dr. Adrian Bronson for proofreading the book.

Contents

1. **Technology and Work in Services: The Relevance of Vulnerable Workers** — 1
   Valeria Cirillo, Matteo Rinaldini, and Maria Enrica Virgillito

2. **Logistics Under Automation and Digitalisation: How Technology *Displaces* Human Work** — 35
   Valeria Cirillo, Francesco S. Massimo, Matteo Rinaldini, and Jacopo Staccioli

3. **Between Empowering and Risk: Organizational Change and Professional Upskilling Through Digital Health Technologies** — 65
   Eleonora Costantini, Marialuisa Divella, Caterina Manicardi, and Matteo Rinaldini

4. **Automation in Cleaning: Why Dirty, Invisible, and Risky Jobs Will Not Be Replaced by Robots Yet** — 97
   Armanda Cetrulo, Caterina Manicardi, and Angelo Moro

5. **Automation, Digitalisation, and Technological Autonomy in the Periphery. A Case Study in the Automotive Complex of Argentina** — 131
   María Celeste Gómez and Carina Borrastero

Index — 165

List of Contributors

Carina Borrastero Centro de Investigaciones en Ciencias Económicas, Universidad Nacional de Córdoba & CONICET, Córdoba, Argentina

Armanda Cetrulo Institute of Economics, Sant'Anna School of Advanced Studies, Pisa, Italy

Valeria Cirillo Department of Political Sciences, University of Bari 'Aldo Moro', Bari, Italy

Eleonora Costantini Marco Biagi Foundation, University of Modena and Reggio Emilia, Modena, Italy

Marialuisa Divella University of Bari 'Aldo Moro', Bari, Italy

María Celeste Gómez Centro de Investigaciones en Ciencias Económicas, Universidad Nacional de Córdoba & CONICET, Córdoba, Argentina

Caterina Manicardi Institute of Economics, Sant'Anna School of Advanced Studies, Pisa, Italy

Francesco S. Massimo Sciences Po, Paris, France; University of Bologna, Bologna, Italy

Angelo Moro University of Modena and Reggio Emilia, Modena, Italy

Matteo Rinaldini University of Modena and Reggio Emilia, Reggio Emilia, Italy

Jacopo Staccioli Catholic University of Milan, Milan, Italy

Maria Enrica Virgillito Institute of Economics, Sant'Anna School of Advanced Studies, Pisa, Italy

List of Figures

Fig. 1.1   Share of employees by selected professions in Italy and Europe (2023). *Source* Labor Force Survey (employees), Eurostat. Selected ISCO codes: Logistics 333, 432; Cleaning 911; Health 321, 532   9

Fig. 1.2   Number of employees and hours worked by selected sectors over time. *Source* Annual National Accounts, Italian National Institute of Statistics. Logistics: warehousing and transport support activities (Nace 52); Cleaning: service activities for buildings and landscape (Nace 81); Health assistance: heath care (Nace 86)   10

Fig. 1.3   Hourly gross real wages of private sector dependent job positions over time by wage percentile. *Source* Annual Register on Wages, Hours and Labor Costs for Individuals and Enterprises (RACLI), Italian National Institute of Statistics. Logistics: warehousing and transport support activities (Nace 52); Cleaning: service activities for buildings and landscape (Nace 81); Health assistance: heath care (Nace 86). The main unit of analysis in the RACLI register is the employee position, defined as the relationship established between an employer and an employee, characterized by a start date and comparable to an employment contract   11

Fig. 1.4   Technologies and work organizational practices by selected professions (2021). *Source* V Survey on Work Quality 2021, Italian National Institute for Public Policy Analysis. Dimensions: (A) **Technology used at work** is built on the question: "*Do you use the following tools in your work?*" *(i) Computers and/or electronic/digital devices (tablet, smartphone); (ii) Internet/email/social media; (iii) Machinery and/or automated systems; (iv) Collaborative robotics (cobots); (v) 3D printers; (vi) Information-sharing systems (Cloud computing); (vii) Systems for simulating production processes (Cloud manufacturing); (ix) Tools for collecting and analyzing large volumes of data (Big Data Analytics).* Variable coding: Variables are coded as 1 if the worker responds with "yes" and 0 if the response is "no". (B) **Teamwork and job rotation** are built upon the question: "*Do you rotate your activities with other workers (e.g., changing positions, departments, job rotation)?*" and "*Do you work in a team, meaning a group with shared responsibilities where you can plan and organize your own work?*". (C) **Autonomy at work** is built upon the question: "*In the context of your work, do you have the opportunity to choose or modify the following?*" *(i) The strategies and objectives to achieve; (ii) The methods and techniques of your work; (iii) The planning of your activities; (iv) Work speed/rhythm.* Variable coding: variables are coded as 1 if the worker responds with "yes, always", and 0 if the response is "sometimes" or "never". (D) **Work surveillance** refers to the question "*Has your company introduced technological innovations in recent years aimed at monitoring and/or evaluating the work activities of employees?*" *(For example, audiovisual systems or other remote-control tools for organizational and production needs, or related to workplace safety and the protection of company assets.).* (E) **Training** refers to the question: "*Have you attended one or more training/upgrading courses relevant to your work in the last year?*". (F) **Mandatory courses** are built upon the question: "*Referring to the course(s) you took in the last year, what was the subject matter covered*". Sample weights applied, ISCO 1 excluded from the analysis for comparability across occupations. Logistics is built on CP (Italian coding for ISCO) 33410, 43120. Cleaning: CP 81410, 81420, 81430. Health: CP 32111, 32112, 32121, 32122, 32123, 32124, 32125, 32126, 32132, 32133, 32141, 32142, 32143, 32144, 32145, 32151, 32152, 32161, 32162, 32170, 53110   14

Fig. 1.5　Percentage of Workers by Technology Used in selected occupations (2021). *Source* V Survey on Work Quality 2021, Italian National Institute for Public Policy Analysis. Question: *"Do you use the following tools in your work?" (i) Computers and/or electronic/digital devices (tablet, smartphone); (ii) Internet/email/social media; (iii) Machinery and/or automated systems; (iv) Collaborative robotics (cobots); (v) 3D printers; (vi) Information-sharing systems (Cloud computing); (vii) Systems for simulating production processes (Cloud manufacturing); (ix) Tools for collecting and analyzing large volumes of data (Big Data Analytics)*. Variable coding: Variables are coded as 1 if the worker responds with "yes" and 0 if the response is "no". Sample weights applied, ISCO 1 excluded from the analysis　15

Fig. 1.6　Share of workers by level of autonomy in work organization and methods (2021). *Source* V Survey on Work Quality 2021, Italian National Institute for Public Policy Analysis. Question: *"In the context of your work, do you have the opportunity to choose or modify the following?"* (i) The strategies and objectives to achieve; (ii) The methods and techniques of your work; (iii) The planning of your activities; (iv) Work speed/rhythm. Variable coding: Variables are coded as 1 if the worker responds with "yes, always", and 0 if the response is "sometimes" or "never". Sample weights applied, ISCO 1 excluded from the analysis　16

List of Tables

Table 1.1	Thousand of employees and share over total economy by selected sectors	8
Table 1.2	Share of dependent workers by selected professions in Italy and Europe and their variation	10
Table 2.1	Automated guided vehicles in the three companies	49
Table 2.2	Labour process restructuring in relation to AGVs	51
Table 2.3	Task reconfiguration in relation to AGVs	55
Table 2.4	Distribution of interviews by company	58
Table 3.1	Summary of technologies and contexts of implementation	79
Table 5.1	Interviews conducted at the plant level	138
Table 5.2	Dimensions of analysis	139
Table 5.3	Interviews on state role dimensions	139

CHAPTER 1

Technology and Work in Services: The Relevance of Vulnerable Workers

Valeria Cirillo, Matteo Rinaldini, and Maria Enrica Virgillito

Abstract This chapter serves as an introduction to the book, which aims to illuminate the experiences of vulnerable workers and the transformation of their work activities through automation and digitalization in the logistics, healthcare, and cleaning industries. It begins with a concise overview of the sectors under study and the workers involved, focusing on key aspects of their work processes to reveal the specific attributes and characteristics of these often-overlooked or "invisible" workers. Drawing on insights from existing literature, key informant interviews, and the authors' analyses, the chapter examines the transformations and impacts

---

V. Cirillo (✉)
Department of Political Sciences, University of Bari 'Aldo Moro', Bari, Italy
e-mail: valeria.cirillo@uniba.it

M. Rinaldini
University of Modena and Reggio Emilia, Reggio Emilia, Italy

M. E. Virgillito
Institute of Economics, Sant'Anna School of Advanced Studies, Pisa, Italy

of technological solutions on vulnerable workers. By intersecting technology and industry, the study provides detailed and nuanced evidence of the ongoing changes shaping work environments in these three sectors.

Keywords Automation · Digitalization · Vulnerable workers · Qualitative analyses · Expert interviews

1.1 The Boundaries of Automation and Digitalization on Labor Processes

Over the last decades, investments in digital and automation technologies have deeply increased, modifying production and distribution processes both in manufacturing and service industries. New digital and automation technologies promise improvements to production and service delivery processes and imply deep changes in the nature and organization of employment. Some part of the literature has highlighted the possible economic advantages stemming from the application of advanced operational technologies due to increased automation, control and interconnectivity, as well as the detrimental effects in terms of quality of work, employment conditions, and even, technological unemployment (Brynjolfsson & Ford, 2015; McAfee, 2014).

The widespread adoption of technology in diverse and multifaceted forms, profoundly influencing both the spheres of production and reproduction, has garnered renewed attention in recent times. The emergence of artifacts embedding certain forms of "intelligent automation"—such as "intelligent robots"—has caused some concerns both in the academic and institutional debates. In recent years, these artifacts have been equipped with learning algorithms able to process an enormous amount of data in real-time and perform functions like classification, prediction, profiling and even interaction with humans. Therefore, a new literature has flourished, providing figures and forecasts about the future of work. The ground is clearly contested between *techno-optimists* and *techno-pessimists*, both in general sharing a strong deterministic perspective on the unfolding of technologies within sectors of activities, firms, and their impact upon labor (Calvino & Virgillito, 2018; Staccioli & Virgillito, 2021). However, comparatively little attention has been devoted to examining the changes in work quality and conditions experienced by so-called "vulnerable" and often "invisible" workers—who are the central focus of this book.

New technologies include a diverse set of solutions and capabilities, encompassing robotics, artificial intelligence, industrial internet of things, big data, cloud computing, augmented reality, additive manufacturing and cybersecurity. Even though it can often be difficult to draw precise lines of demarcation, these are different technologies subject to convergence and re-combinatory adoption among technology users (Cirillo et al., 2024). In fact, it can be hard in quantitative and qualitative types of research to assess the exact demarcation between automation, digitalization and interconnection of devices.

Digitalization, robotization/automation, and interconnectivity can be interrelated; for instance, the automotive sector provides clear-cut examples of these tendencies. Digitally enabled machines aimed at automating and interconnecting specific phases of production and distribution processes may have deep consequences on work that can be better understood at the level of tasks more than jobs. In fact, the major difference with the past, as compared to the previous technological waves, concerns both the pervasiveness as well as the number of tasks that digital devices and digitally equipped machines are now able to perform, some of which were previously believed to be an exclusive prerogative of humans (Cirillo et al., 2021a, 2021b). Worker's tasks are in fact the fundamental entities which can be reshaped (or substituted) by digital machines and robots impacting labor processes and work practices.

The attention toward tasks more than jobs is not new in the scientific debate. Indeed, the dominant framework for the explanation of humane-machine relationship relies on the so-called task-based approach. Popularized by Autor et al. (2003), it considers the bundle of tasks executed by each worker as the most important dimension upon which technological change and, particularly in earlier versions, the use of computers at work, shapes the dynamics of occupations. Notably, the routine vs. non-routine dichotomy has become mainstream in economic literature (*Routine Biased Technical Change*—RBTC). The underlying idea is that some human tasks can be more easily substituted by technological change, represented by the use of computers, while others are less so. The degree of substitutability depends on the amount of codified knowledge required to execute a given task.

However, the RBTC approach has also been criticized due to its mere technical view of the production, seen as a mechanical process of transforming inputs into outputs disregarding both human agency and social aspects of production processes (Fernández-Macías & Hurley, 2017). Tasks are understood as discrete units of work activity producing actual output and susceptible to replacement. Indeed, the underlying element relied upon by both RBTC and the task-based approach is the existence of a given degree of substitutability between labor and capital.

Another criticism of the RBTC approach concerns the excessive importance attributed to the routine content of tasks and the undervaluing of other fundamental dimensions of the work process. For instance, Pfeiffer (2016, 2018) emphasizes how a long tradition of qualitative studies has widely demonstrated the continuing importance of workers' physical/sensory perceptions and their ability to establish empathetic relationships with the social and material context in which they are embedded, even in highly automated and digital work environments. The activation of this set of exclusively human abilities is defined as "subjectifying work action" referring to the broad spectrum of abilities and knowledge that cannot be fully subsumed within a formal work process.[1] These actions are rooted not in logic or rationality but in the use of the body and its five senses, enabling workers not only to enact forms of resistance but also to understand the concrete work processes they are involved in, manage unexpected events, prevent work process interruptions (or disintegrations), and generate innovations (Pfeiffer, 2014). The development of these practical abilities and knowledge requires time as work experience and the conditions needed for its enhancement in work processes are important (Pfeiffer & Suphan, 2015). All this points to both work activities conducted in "analogic work environments" and work activities carried out in complex, hyper-connected, and abstract work environments driven by intensive use of digital and automation technologies, regardless of the routine nature of tasks. Therefore, the issue posed by the adoption of new technologies is not just the substitutability of routine tasks and their identification and measurement, but rather how the use of new technologies is accompanied by processes of acceleration of the "subjectification of work action". The latter represents an essential condition for achieving what the narrative of the "Fourth Industrial Revolution"

---

[1] The latter represents an interpretation of the Marxian dialectical pair "living labouring capacity (use value)"/"labour power (exchange value)" (Pfeiffer, 2014).

promises: economic development, greater efficiency, enhanced innovation capabilities, and improved extrinsic and intrinsic working conditions (Kagermann et al., 2013). By increasing productivity, both automation and digitalization can *displace* labor, although compensation mechanisms should be carefully taken into account. Job losses might occur but more importantly changes in tasks and skills need to be accommodated through work organization. Additionally, automation and digitalization affect work organization in more direct ways. Digital technologies are quite literally technologies of control and monitoring. They tend to standardize work tasks and centralize control (Wood, 2021).

Given the complexity of the nature of work, the degree of substitutability between humans and machines should be evaluated considering the intersection of several other elements beyond technical feasibility and relative efficiency gains, such as existing technological trajectories, the amount of codified and non-codified knowledge, the relevance of organizational routines and practices, and institutional factors. All these elements deeply influence the relation between jobs, tasks and technologies, and, of course, automation (Cetrulo et al., 2020; Montobbio et al., 2024). Overall, a full understanding of the technological complexity underling robotics and automation is still lacking, most of all when looking at the consequences on work and vulnerable workers.

Much of the current research efforts devoted to study the effects of technological transformation on the world of work are focused on the manufacturing sector, while scarce attention has been devoted toward the study of services. More recently, artificial intelligence and other computational breakthroughs have also become increasingly relevant to the service sector, which nowadays employs the largest share of workforce. All these elements motivate the need to investigate the consequences of automation in services. To pursue this goal, this book intends to investigate the transformation that the labor process in selected industries of the service sector has undertaken in the last years.

The book delves into the analysis of three specific sectors, namely logistics, healthcare and cleaning. The three sectors are of relevance because of the specific unfolding of the technology upon tasks and competences often thought to be distant from technologies and because of the composition and type of the workforce employed. The three sectors are investigated by means of a qualitative workplace-industry analysis conducted in Italy. In addition, a chapter of the book is devoted to study the more classic automotive industry, however located in one of the most important automotive complex in a peripheral country in South America, Argentina. The choice of the industry-country design allows us to address a series of themes that will be cross-cutting along the entire book, particularly the theme of technological dependence and autonomy in decision choice to adopt and use the technology and the theme of technological integration. Heterogeneity in the institutional settings that the book embraces is informative about the importance, or lack of it, of the social actors and institutions in the process at stake. In fact, by covering different industries located in two countries, we are able to identify a distinct role that institutions and industrial relations undertake. Paralleling traditional core versus peripheral workplaces, in terms of their organizations and institutional architectures, increases the power of analysis and implications deriving from the empirical findings.

Industrial relations in the service sector are notoriously informal, with trade unions—partly due to the nature of the work under study—lacking significant power or influence to impact the bargaining process surrounding the introduction of new technologies. In addition, institutional forms such as national legal requirements and constraints in sectors like cleaning and healthcare, or alternatively, because of the role of local actors like in the case of the Argentinian industrial complex, might play a relevant role in affecting the relationship of technologies with workers. The role of the state and local regulations will emerge with reference to three industries, particularly the healthcare sector, historically characterized by a private–public nexus that influences the way in which work is performed and service provisions are administered. It also emerges in the cleaning sector, characterized by social clauses that create normative limits to contractual regulation, and in the automotive industry in Argentina, characterized by the active role assumed by local actors and national institutions.

Moreover, not only collective institutions, but also private multinational corporations (MNCs) and their strategies will take center stage and be critically examined. Their role will be particularly prominent in the logistics industry, where the relationship between technological autonomy or dependence and its effects on labor process restructuring become evident. MNCs are capable of deploying a broad spectrum of strategies, balancing decisions on technological adoption, market positioning, internal labor practices, and integration with production chains involving clients and suppliers. The manner in which MNCs engage with technology often reflects their market positioning. They may fully own and develop the technologies they use, curate portfolios of diverse technologies sourced from various players, or construct internal architectures to integrate these solutions effectively. Alternatively, MNCs—and particularly their subsidiary plants—may largely rely on technological solutions determined elsewhere, often at the headquarters of the parent company. This approach may demonstrate limited attention to localized development trajectories or adoption paths tailored to specific internal needs.

The nature of technological dependence or autonomy and the strategic choices made significantly influence the world of work, shaping labor process restructuring, the reorganization of workplaces, and the emergence of new hierarchies, roles, and functions. This is precisely the focus of this book.

In the following Sections, we specifically focus on workers and technological transformations occurring in the three service sectors, leaving aside an exhaustive discussion of the manufacturing industry, given that the latter has been widely covered by the literature. The interested reader may refer to Cirillo et al. (2021b), among others. With reference to specific themes intersecting manufacturing labor and technological deployment in peripheral areas, the reader should make reference to Chapter 5.

1.2 Vulnerable Workers Under Automation and Digitalization

To motivate the relevance and peculiarity of the industries under study and the workers involved therein, we give a concise representation of their importance, in terms of employment absorption, pays, and work organization. We focus on some aspects of the work process to appreciate the specific attributes and characteristics of these workers, often defined as vulnerable or "invisible" workers.

The three service sectors in Italy, the reference country of the book, collectively employ approximately 15% of the total workforce, representing around 3 million workers (Table 1.1). Notably, healthcare assistance alone accounts for over 8% of total employment, while cleaning and logistics contribute 4% and 2%, respectively.

Focusing on specific professions within these sectors (Fig. 1.1), Labor Force Survey statistics reveal that in 2023, *domestic, hotel, and office cleaners and helpers* alone made up over 4% of total employees in Italy, compared to 3.5% in Europe. Similarly, *personal care workers in health*

Table 1.1 Thousand of employees and share over total economy by selected sectors

	2019	2020	2021	2022
Logistics	385.9	386	398.2	408.9
	(2.0%)	(2.1%)	(2.1%)	(2.1%)
Cleaning	840	812.8	823.7	835.8
	(4.4%)	(4.3%)	(4.3%)	(4.3%)
Health assistance	1596.5	1610.5	1627.2	1650.3
	(8.4%)	(8.6%)	(8.5%)	(8.4%)

Source Annual National Accounts (employees), Italian National Institute of Statistics. Logistics: warehousing and transport support activities (Nace 52); Cleaning: service activities for buildings and landscape (Nace 81); Health assistance: heath care (Nace 86)

services accounted for 3.8% in Italy, compared to 2.4% in Europe. In the logistics industry, *material-recording and transport clerks* represented about 2.4% of the workforce in 2023, totaling more than 700,000 workers. Such numbers highlight the fact that in the industries under investigation, although populated by a wide range of professional categories, the bottom-end occupations are those that mostly account for the employment dynamics. Moreover, two of these sectors (health and cleaning) show patterns of gender sectoral segregation with an incidence of women around 70%.

The numbers of people employed in the sectors have significantly grown over time (Fig. 1.2), both in terms of the hours worked and number of employees. The exception to this trend was the COVID-19 crisis in 2020, which caused a sharp decline in hours worked across all sectors—though employment levels were less affected, likely due to the government-mandated ban on layoffs. Over time, all three sectors have expanded. In logistics and cleaning, hours worked have grown faster than employment, whereas in healthcare and assistance, the opposite trend is observed. In general, the three sectors show high vulnerability and cycling dynamics and tend to be exposed more than the average employees to working hour volatility and corresponding vulnerable pays. Distinctly, employment in healthcare and assistance is growing faster than hours worked, likely due to the prevalence of part-time and low-intensity forms of work in these industries.

According to Labor Force Survey data, the number of personal care workers in health services in Italy grew by nearly 40% between 2012 and

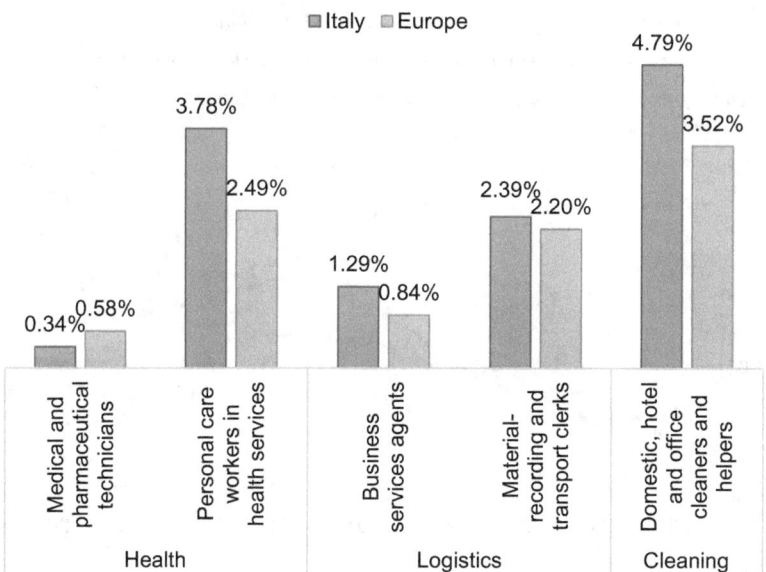

Fig. 1.1 Share of employees by selected professions in Italy and Europe (2023). *Source* Labor Force Survey (employees), Eurostat. Selected ISCO codes: Logistics 333, 432; Cleaning 911; Health 321, 532

2023, compared to 18% in Europe (see Table 1.2). The incidence of part-time in these professions is about 70%, well-above other professions. The high incidence of part-time and the coexistence of contracts with a high variability across weeks are two symptoms of vulnerability. The latter arises in presence of jobs whose contractual regulation is not able to guarantee temporal continuity and stable work intensity (ISTAT, 2022).

The vulnerability of the workers employed in such industries is clearly expressed by the recorded wage penalty, although their numbers keep growing in terms of jobs. Median hourly wage for workers (job category) in logistics, cleaning, and healthcare is below the economy-wide median, at a modest €11 per hour (Fig. 1.3). The cleaning sector is the one experiencing the highest penalties. The hourly wage is even lower at the bottom 10th percentile, compared to the total economy, while the healthcare sector shows higher bottom wages. Logistics has recorded some improvement over time.

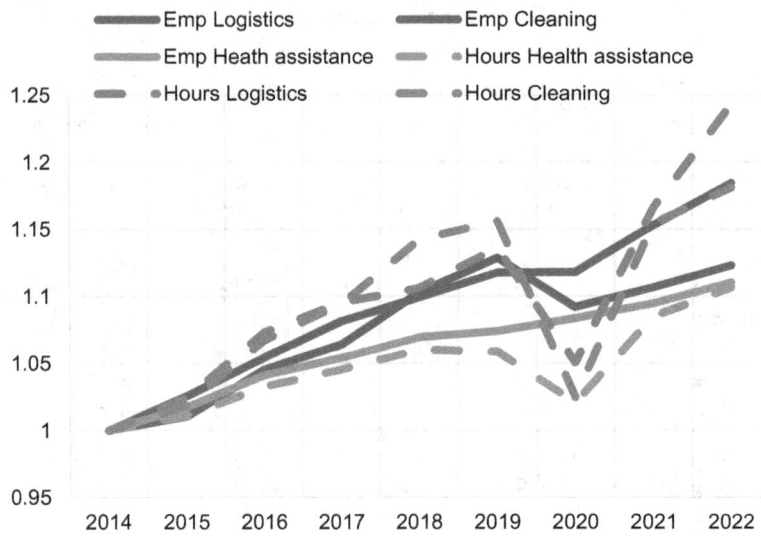

Fig. 1.2 Number of employees and hours worked by selected sectors over time. *Source* Annual National Accounts, Italian National Institute of Statistics. Logistics: warehousing and transport support activities (Nace 52); Cleaning: service activities for buildings and landscape (Nace 81); Health assistance: heath care (Nace 86)

Table 1.2 Share of dependent workers by selected professions in Italy and Europe and their variation

		Var % 2012—2023		Share 2023	
		IT (%)	EU (%)	IT (%)	EU (%)
Health	Medical and pharmaceutical technicians	21.2	12.7	0.34	0.58
	Personal care workers in health services	40.4	18.2	3.78	2.49
Logistics	Business services agents	34.1	41.1	1.29	0.84
	Material-recording and transport clerks	3.2	−7.1	2.39	2.20
Cleaning	Domestic, hotel and office cleaners and helpers	−11.8	−8.7	4.79	3.52

Source Labor Force Survey (employees), Eurostat. Selected ISCO codes: Logistics 333, 432; Cleaning 911; Health 321, 532

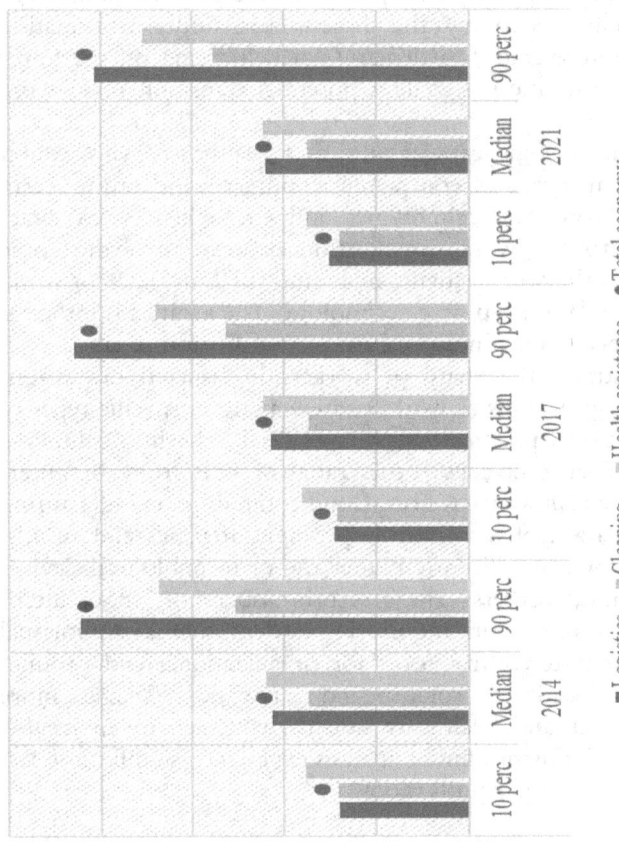

Fig. 1.3 Hourly gross real wages of private sector dependent job positions over time by wage percentile. *Source* Annual Register on Wages, Hours and Labor Costs for Individuals and Enterprises (RACLI), Italian National Institute of Statistics. Logistics: warehousing and transport support activities (Nace 52); Cleaning: service activities for buildings and landscape (Nace 81); Health assistance: heath care (Nace 86). The main unit of analysis in the RACLI register is the employee position, defined as the relationship established between an employer and an employee, characterized by a start date and comparable to an employment contract

At the top of the distribution, the wage gap between the cleaning sector and the overall economy widens significantly. Cleaning workers at the top of the wage distribution earn, on average, €12–€13 per hour. In contrast, workers in logistics at the top earn, on average, €20 per hour, which is comparable to the broader economy. Healthcare workers earn slightly less, with an average of €17 per hour. Despite the poor wage prospects in the Italian economy, the three sectors under investigation remain notably below average, particularly when focusing on the lower end of the wage distribution, signaling potential transition to in work poverty.

How do workers in logistics, cleaning, and healthcare, who exhibit vulnerable patterns in terms of contractual conditions and wages, carry out their work? How do technologies influence their work practices? We delve into the work organization process, involving some specific attributes of the work activity, including rhythms, pace of work, autonomy, and the relationship with technology. The analysis is informative of the nexus between technological usage and division of labor.

Figure 1.4 illustrates the share of workers in selected professions employing technological tools at work, and engaging in specific types of work and organizational practices. More specifically, the first column—technology at work—encompasses a broad range of tools, from computers and social media to collaborative robots, cloud computing, manufacturing systems, and big data analytics. Not surprisingly, logistics and healthcare professions show a significantly higher use of technological devices compared to cleaning workers. These sectors also report more intensive usage and exposure to work monitoring devices, such as audiovisual systems or other remote-control tools for organizational and production needs. Notably, besides job rotation and teamwork—which are more widespread in logistics and healthcare due to work activity in itself—workers in the three industries under analysis experience significantly less autonomy compared to other professions.

1 TECHNOLOGY AND WORK IN SERVICES: THE RELEVANCE ... 13

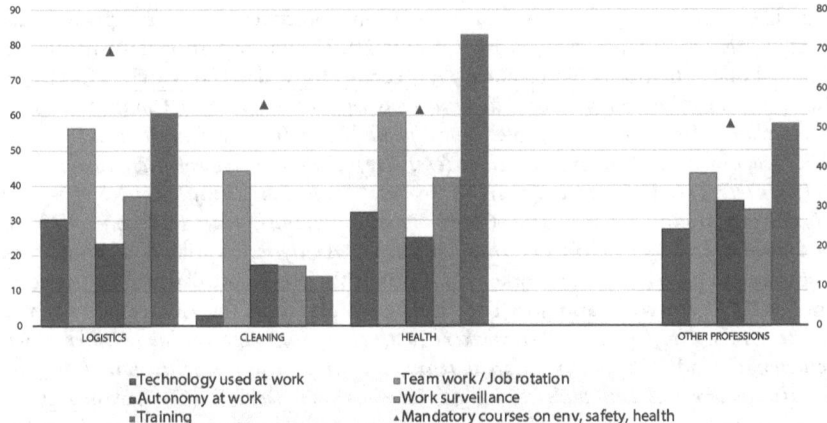

■ Technology used at work ■ Team work / Job rotation
■ Autonomy at work ■ Work surveillance
■ Training ▲ Mandatory courses on env, safety, health

◀**Fig. 1.4** Technologies and work organizational practices by selected professions (2021). *Source* V Survey on Work Quality 2021, Italian National Institute for Public Policy Analysis. Dimensions: (A) **Technology used at work** is built on the question: *"Do you use the following tools in your work?"* *(i) Computers and/or electronic/digital devices (tablet, smartphone); (ii) Internet/email/social media; (iii) Machinery and/or automated systems; (iv) Collaborative robotics (cobots); (v) 3D printers; (vi) Information-sharing systems (Cloud computing); (vii) Systems for simulating production processes (Cloud manufacturing); (ix) Tools for collecting and analyzing large volumes of data (Big Data Analytics).* Variable coding: Variables are coded as 1 if the worker responds with "yes" and 0 if the response is "no". (B) **Teamwork and job rotation** are built upon the question: *"Do you rotate your activities with other workers (e.g., changing positions, departments, job rotation)?"* and *"Do you work in a team, meaning a group with shared responsibilities where you can plan and organize your own work?".* (C) **Autonomy at work** is built upon the question: *"In the context of your work, do you have the opportunity to choose or modify the following?" (i) The strategies and objectives to achieve; (ii) The methods and techniques of your work; (iii) The planning of your activities; (iv) Work speed/rhythm.* Variable coding: variables are coded as 1 if the worker responds with "yes, always", and 0 if the response is "sometimes" or "never". (D) **Work surveillance** refers to the question *"Has your company introduced technological innovations in recent years aimed at monitoring and/or evaluating the work activities of employees?" (For example, audiovisual systems or other remote-control tools for organizational and production needs, or related to workplace safety and the protection of company assets.).* (E) **Training** refers to the question: *"Have you attended one or more training/upgrading courses relevant to your work in the last year?".* (F) **Mandatory courses** are built upon the question: *"Referring to the course(s) you took in the last year, what was the subject matter covered".* Sample weights applied, ISCO 1 excluded from the analysis for comparability across occupations. Logistics is built on CP (Italian coding for ISCO) 33410, 43120. Cleaning: CP 81410, 81420, 81430. Health: CP 32111, 32112, 32121, 32122, 32123, 32124, 32125, 32126, 32132, 32133, 32141, 32142, 32143, 32144, 32145, 32151, 32152, 32161, 32162, 32170, 53110

Moreover, workers in logistics and healthcare are more likely to undergo training than those in cleaning and other sectors. However, a large portion of this training is focused on mandatory courses related to the environment, safety, and health, rather than on the development of workers specific skill sets.

Figure 1.5 shows that healthcare and logistics occupations are more intensively marked by the use of digital devices compared to other professions and the cleaning sector as well. However, more basic applications—such as internet, email, and social media—are more commonly used than advanced technologies like cloud computing. Logistics workers, in particular, stand out for their higher usage of cloud manufacturing, big data analytics, and collaborative robots compared to other fields. Health-related professions, meanwhile, register a more intensive use of machinery and/or automated systems, along with cloud computing.

Such type of evidence will be then specifically investigated into the case study analyses conducted in the following chapters. It has to be noted that the exposure to the use of specific technologies across the three categories is different, while similar traits are the low degree of autonomy and a rigid and prescribed rhythm of work.

In fact, Fig. 1.6 shows a rigid hierarchy endured by workers across professions, with healthcare, logistics, and cleaning workers consistently

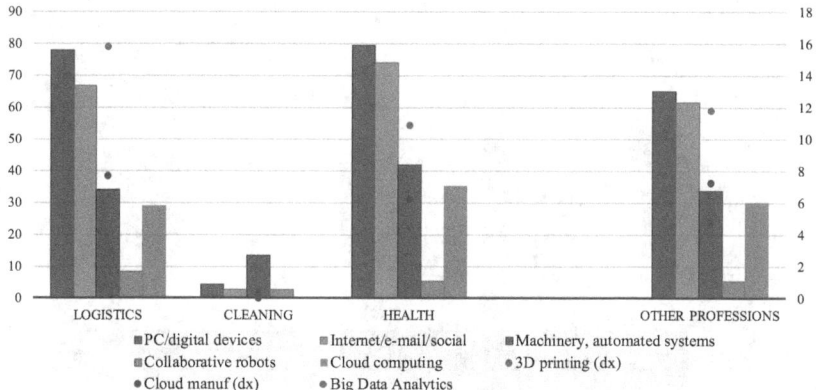

Fig. 1.5 Percentage of Workers by Technology Used in selected occupations (2021). *Source* V Survey on Work Quality 2021, Italian National Institute for Public Policy Analysis. Question: *"Do you use the following tools in your work?" (i) Computers and/or electronic/digital devices (tablet, smartphone); (ii) Internet/email/social media; (iii) Machinery and/or automated systems; (iv) Collaborative robotics (cobots); (v) 3D printers; (vi) Information-sharing systems (Cloud computing); (vii) Systems for simulating production processes (Cloud manufacturing); (ix) Tools for collecting and analyzing large volumes of data (Big Data Analytics).* Variable coding: Variables are coded as 1 if the worker responds with "yes" and 0 if the response is "no". Sample weights applied, ISCO 1 excluded from the analysis

falling below the average level of autonomy observed in other occupations. This is particularly evident when it comes to setting work strategies and objectives, even on a day-to-day basis. Workers in these fields have limited freedom in choosing which tools and methods to use or in determining the order of tasks. Cleaning workers, in particular, experience very restricted autonomy: fewer than one-quarter have any say in the work process, except in deciding the speed and rhythm of their tasks. Looking at the time variation of working conditions (not shown here), there has been a significant *decline* in the autonomy that workers have in performing their tasks, especially regarding work methods, techniques, and activity planning.

The presentation of the characteristic traits of the work process under the industries of studies allows us to identify that workers investigated in this book are vulnerable and invisible. With invisible work, taking the

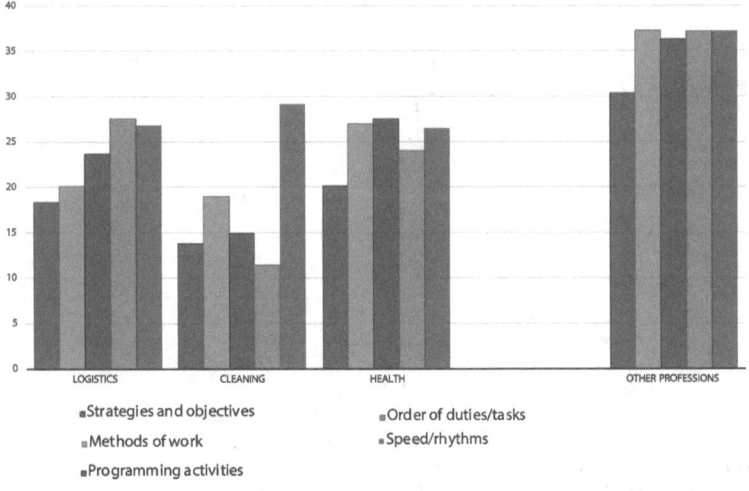

Fig. 1.6 Share of workers by level of autonomy in work organization and methods (2021). *Source* V Survey on Work Quality 2021, Italian National Institute for Public Policy Analysis. Question: "*In the context of your work, do you have the opportunity to choose or modify the following?*" (i) The strategies and objectives to achieve; (ii) The methods and techniques of your work; (iii) The planning of your activities; (iv) Work speed/rhythm. Variable coding: Variables are coded as 1 if the worker responds with "yes, always", and 0 if the response is "sometimes" or "never". Sample weights applied, ISCO 1 excluded from the analysis

perspective by Hatton (2017) we include all the types of economic activities that are subject to forms of invisibility because of economic devaluation: "*'invisible work' as labour that is economically devalued through three intersecting sociological mechanisms—here identified as cultural, legal and spatial mechanisms of invisibility—which operate in different ways and to different degrees*" (Hatton, 2017, p. 337).

One of the aims of this book is exactly shedding new lights on the forms of labor that are not considered worthy to be investigated when looking at the transformation induced by technologies. However, as each chapter will show, the interaction between invisible labor, automation and digitalization is not trivial and far from deterministic deskilling expectations. One example, as will be made clear, is found in Chapter 3, which focuses on the healthcare sector. In this case, new technologies are reshaping hierarchies in favor of lower professional categories, creating a new hybrid role for nurses who are now able to perform tasks that were previously in the domain of doctors. As a result, to fully understand the processes at play, the empirical setting intersects with technology, industries, and the labor process, highlighting specific patterns of change.

1.3 Methodology

Workplace and industry studies paint a detailed picture of the current dynamics usually neglected by pure quantitative approaches. At the time this research began, large-scale and representative databases able to integrate firm-level information with labor market dynamics detailed by skills and tasks were not still available. Furthermore, there are very few surveys able to capture work organizational aspects and industrial relations related to the adoption of technologies. Therefore, this book has benefited from a qualitative approach based on the administration of semi-structured interviews to specific professional figures operating within the companies.

The main objective of this book is to investigate the impact of the automation of processes on work organization, tasks, working conditions and industrial relations in specific workplaces located in Italy and Argentina by focusing on the adoption of technologies linked to automation and digitalization.

The research focused on technology and work in services has been structured in two phases. The first one aimed at selecting a shortlist of potential cases (i.e., companies/organizations where the technology has been adopted). This meant carrying out several informal interviews (including in-person meeting and video calling) with representatives of the companies and key informants. More than twenty interviews have been realized during this phase. These interviews have been useful both to collect general information on the sectoral diffusion of the technologies under consideration and to deepen the knowledge of the macro-impacts of these technologies on economic and industrial processes. The identification of adopters has required an accurate strategy for case selection aimed at identifying a list of "adopters" and among them, selecting cases to be included in the analysis.

The second phase involved both a visit to the selected companies/ organizations, and the realization of semi-structured interviews with several professional figures, including different profiles such as HR management, trade union representative, a technology specialist (the person in charge of implementing or managing the technology) and workers in key occupations affected by the technology under consideration. The general interview template was built to allow for comparability across the different company cases. Such a general template (a grid of the questions to follow during the interviews) focused on several macro areas of interest, such as the impact of the technology on the economic process; the impact of the technology on work organization; the effects on tasks and job quality. Once the cases were defined, the general interview template was adapted according both to the type of establishment selected and the profile of the interviewees (one for HR manager and technology specialist, one for trade union representative, and one for workers). Moreover, the visits to the companies/organizations allowed the research group to collect data through direct observation of both the technology under study and the work processes involving their use. In parallel, the research team carried out a desk analysis. A total of nine workplaces were analyzed—six through in-person visits and interviews, and three through online interviews due to COVID-19 restrictions. The fieldwork lasted from July 2021 to February 2022.

Similarly to the Italian fieldwork, the research on technology and work at the Argentinian automotive plant was structured in two phases as well. The first phase focused on data collection and several in-person visits to the plant, which allowed for the observation of adopted technologies, production processes, and the behavior of the workers involved. The second phase included additional focus meetings, during which the research team conducted five in-depth, in-person interviews with executives, supervisors, workers, union representatives (at both the firm and territorial levels), as well as one representative from an employers' association. The template of interviews was similar to the Italian one. However, in the case of the Argentinian research activities, just one specific plant was analyzed, therefore skipping the phase of the definition of the list of adopters. Given the different sector, the country, and the relevance of the factory under investigation, the definition of the adopter was quite straightforward. The fieldwork lasted from August 2023 to May 2024.

A total of fifty-nine interviews were conducted in Italy and seven in Argentina (about 45 minutes of face-to-face anonymous interviews, most of them on site, some online). All the interviews were recorded and later transcribed.

A content analysis of each single interview was carried out: interview transcripts were analyzed and coded in order to move from more abstract contents toward more concrete ones and to shed light on the following key dimensions: (i) impact on work organization, workflows, and processes; (ii) impact on employment and working conditions; (iii) impact on occupational composition, job profiles and task content; (iv) other potential effects on the company and workers.

The informative material and data collected were analysed through an iterative approach, whereby the research group went back and forth from data to theory and vice versa. The use of multiple points of view allowed the research team to triangulate the data, thus providing stronger substantiation of the emerging constructs (Alvesson & Karreman, 2011; Eisenhardt, 1989).

1.4 Technology and the Transformation of the Work Process

Below, we detail the list of technological artifacts for each specific industry under investigation in the following chapters. In addition, we lay out the effects expected in terms of the transformation of the work process, referring to task reconfiguration and professional profiles. Results reported include literature findings, key informant interviews and authors' expectations. The technological solutions that are studied are expected to exert notable transformations and impacts for vulnerable workers, and this hypothesis will be confirmed throughout the book. Intersecting technology and industry allows us to gather detailed and nuanced evidence on the ongoing transformations.

1.4.1 Logistics and Warehouses

Automated (or Autonomously) Guided Vehicles (AGVs) are mobile robots used in industrial and in non-manufacturing applications to automatically move materials from one point to another. While the older versions of AGVs stop when in front of an obstacle and usually follow a pre-set route by reading special floor markings, the latest models combine sophisticated sensors and navigation systems. They are usually applied in two types of operations: autonomous loading and transport, and assisted order picking. Logistics activities can be conducted inside manufacturing firms or in-house warehouses, while third-party logistics (3PL) are firms which implement so-called technological and business solutions to optimize firm production flow with external warehouses.

Three obstacles have been identified with respect to the adoption of automation (Gutelius & Theodore, 2019): (i) cost-sensitivity in a low value-added phase; (ii) high variability in clients; (iii) high flexibility in labor hiring.

With respect to the first set of factors, it should be acknowledged that 3PL firms operate on very stringent profit margins; it is a very cost-sensitive segment performing those phases, as picking and distributing, that manufacturing producers usually wish to outsource. Prices are still the major determinants to obtain outsourcing and contract attribution, therefore, cheap labor is always more convenient with respect to costly automation. The second set of reasons has to do with high variability in clients and short-lasting contracts: given that 3PL operates with low profit margins, they tend to accept a wide variety of contracts, lasting from three to five years, from heterogeneous industry clients, to food processing to automotive industries, to pharmaceuticals. The high variability of managed products and the short duration of contracts imply that warehouses are not organized so far in a standardised manner, in such a way that stringent automated processes can be easily implemented.

Lastly, high flexibility in labor hiring represents a further obstacle to automation. The segment is populated by enterprises relying on a small share of employed personnel, and massive use of sub-contracts, tenders and sub-tenders to outsource to fourth-party organisations, often "cooperatives", which do not employ personnel directly either. The overuse of cheap labor, temporary hired on demand, allows to perfectly meet the needs of just-in-time flows required by clients of 3PL. This cascade structure puts stress on the ultimate segment of the logistics phase, that is temporary workers, often migrant and relatively weak in terms of contractual negotiation, distributed by temporary staffing agencies, or even by informal trucks' owners, to different routes and operations.

To sum up, obstacles to adoption are deep and diverse. They include technical unfeasibility, high variability of clients,[2] short-lasting contracts for 3PL, institutional factors (e.g., automation must be discussed with unions and changes should be negotiated in the mark of the legal framework imposed by the National Collective Agreement); cheap and abundant labor force performing labor-intensive activities relatively hard to automate inhibits technological, risky, investments.

Against this background, the business model of firms operating in the 3PL has rapidly changed over time, since the logistics sector itself has undertaken several restructuring phases over the last years. One important transformation concerns the timing of shipping and delivering. As Amazon is a leader in the automation of warehouses, TNT (ex-Traco) has played an important role in the reorganization of the timescale of shipping and delivery operations, changing the timescale to five working days delivery and forcing other companies to adapt both with respect to cost cutting (in picking and delivery) and number of workers per truck—from two (driver plus one) to only one worker (driver). When TNT introduced this important change, even Domenichelli, the first leader in the sector, closed down because it could not withstand the competition. In fact, in contrast with other industries, profits in logistics have always been relatively low, at least before the outbreak of COVID-19, ranging from -1 to 8% (*Earnings before interest and taxes*, PwC, 2016). However, even in this sector a huge heterogeneity of firm performance needs to be accounted: while carriers can be close to zero profit, large courier/express companies are the most profitable groups, even reaching double-digit profit margins (PwC, 2016).

Another relevant transformation of the sector has to do with the introduction of home delivery (to the final consumer) which is led by Amazon; TNT and Bartolini followed the same path. These changes have strongly affected the business model of firms operating in the logistics sector and their technological choices. In fact, logistics firms have started to outsource work to cooperatives and more often to rely on temporary agency work instead on direct employees. The availability of a cheap

---

[2] The introduction of AGVs implies physical reorganization of the warehouse and imposes a reorganization of multi-brand storehouses.

labor force has hindered the realization of costly investments, such as those related to technology, with the exception of companies like Amazon and few market leaders. However, the outbreak of COVID-19 imposed a further reorganization of the sector: since consumers now rely on online shopping, this has increased both range and volume demands on supply chains augmenting delivery speed and service levels (PwC, 2020).

In terms of changes in occupational structure and task reconfiguration due to technological adoption, key informants refer that in logistics, automation has not been associated so far with labor replacement; whereas technologies introduced, such as sorters and RFID, have led to an intensification of work more than purely a labor-displacing effect. Although so far, a pure labor-displacing effect has not been detected, there are several tasks affected by the introduction of AGVs. For instance, these are: (i) tasks performed by operators concerning picking-type of activities which have been automated by the machine—AGVs are designed to replace traditional forklifts[3]; (ii) tasks performed by operators concerning management of inventories, i.e., the operations of governance of the flow of supply and handling of materials; (iii) tasks performed by operators concerning material handling operations and transport of material directly to the place where it is to be used, i.e., the transport of materials to storage areas, support for just-in-time shipments, delivery of work-in-process components to production lines and transport of finished products to shipping areas.

According to Alumotion, one of the provider of AGVs, the latter can replace a task carried out by a lift truck (run by an operator), and the average annual cost of using AGVs is about $1/3$ of the average annual cost of using lift trucks. If, on the other hand, AGVs replace or reallocate operators' activities, labor costs can be reduced and productivity can be increased, as staff need breaks while self-driving vehicles do not.

In terms of working conditions, the application of AGVs should allow employees to focus on high-value activities, not deliveries, and to avoid heavy loads (this is advertised by tech providers). However, the manual nature of much warehouse work, entailing repetitive movements, awkward lifting and moving positions, and a fast-paced work environment, together put workers at risk of injury (Gutelius & Theodore,

---

[3] Picking is the process of collecting customer orders and sending the goods to another warehouse (e.g., distribution center) or other sale-points. On average it accounts for 55% of the total cost of the warehouse.

2019). Work intensification has been recorded in our research, even though some technologies could alleviate the most arduous tasks of warehouse work (such as heavy lifting). This likely will be coupled with attempts to increase the workload and pace of work, with new methods of monitoring workers; simplification of aspects of warehouse work by breaking a job into subtasks; introduction of new professional figures meant at performing quality control and maintenance of the technology.

The findings from Chapter 2 regarding the logistics sector align with those presented by Gutelius and Theodore (2019) in the context of the US. Automated Guided Vehicles (AGVs) are increasingly used to replace forklift drivers, who are among the highest-paid nonsupervisory workers due to their specialized skill sets. More specifically, forklift driving has been restructured into distinct subtasks, with the more easily automatable activities removing the need for skilled labor. This shift has led to the *displacement* of logistics operators, a topic that will be discussed in detail in Chapter 2.

1.4.2 Remote Monitoring in Healthcare

The healthcare system has developed some technological solutions in the past ten years to implement remote patient monitoring. However, before the outbreak of COVID-19 what goes under the heading of telemedicine did encounter a series of obstacles, mainly organizational and technological barriers. The spreading of the pandemic has led some hospitals and elderly residences to reconsider the possibility of adopting remote monitoring systems.

In general, an aging and lonely population, the dismantling of territorial assistance, the gradual process of centralization versus big, multipurpose hospitals, the needs of continuous monitoring of chronic diseases have led toward a gradual reconsideration of more structured programs of telemedicine, also introducing fees and payment systems before unknown.

The state-of-the-art technologies in healthcare monitoring include: digital processes, monitoring patient parameters, human sensors and wearables; home-based visits by means of virtual platforms; robotic devices used to replace human activity in environments exposed to infections and diseases, particularly for meal deliveries and cleaning; artificial intelligence to provide assisted diagnosis by means of machine learning algorithms trained on the basis of large-scale datasets, aggregating information on patients' parameters.

Technological adoption is overall in an uptake phase in the healthcare sector, with a high level of variability ranging from artificial intelligence and service robots as the least diffused technologies, while remote monitoring by means of wearables, sensors and the provision of telemedicine looks to be more widespread. On one hand, the obstacles to adoption are deep and diverse. Among them the literature, (Litwin, 2020), and key informants identified (i) pricing policies of telemedicine; (ii) difficulties in identifying the pool of patients to be telemonitored; (iii) strong reorganizational needs to re-arrange shifts and intra-day working activities; (iv) software integration among diverse units such as central healthcare divisions, hospitals, private clinics, elderly residences; (v) reliance upon caregivers; (vi) digital divide to ensure assistance to patients; (vii) fragmentation between those who decide to undertake a technological innovation (financial and ownership actors) and those who are going to define whether that technology is actually worthy to be deployed (medical and care giver personnel).

On the other hand, the main drivers for introducing monitoring devices range from the possibility to increase access to healthcare monitoring to reducing hospitals stress and disease prevention to productivity gains.

Although the field of telemedicine has lagged far behind in Italy and telerobotic medicine is almost non-existent, expectations about adoption are positive compared to initial experimentation projects, and the pandemic has greatly accelerated the adoption process. The projection on the healthcare facility system is that dialogue and visits at home might have a huge impact and, if widely adopted, might allow hospitals to unload working rhythms and urgency accesses. More specifically, there are several applications such as: (i) telemedicine, including telemonitoring, involving the detection of parameters from patients digitally sent to the health center; (ii) active transmission by the patient: patients in quarantine or isolation transmit some parameters of their physical state; (iii) televisit or teleconsultation: the patient uses its own tools to access a remote visit without moving, that is, home-made visits with information transfer. The latter is used for patients located in rural and mountain areas who have been provided with devices that transmit parameters to hospitals and GP—general practitioner.

In all cases described above, the adoption of remote monitoring devices entailing the possibility of detecting parameters from patients digitally sent to the health center and the use of sensors that transmit to the health facility are expected to affect tasks performed by doctors, medical staff in general, and caregivers.

By allowing doctors to be constantly updated about the health status of their patients, the employment of remote monitoring devices certainly affects their work organization and workload. Indeed, these latter do not longer need to visit all their patients in person to get the information necessary and, thus, can just focus in-person visits on the most critical cases.

However, with respect to doctors, telemedicine and remote monitoring devices could in theory imply the creation of a new task concerning the evaluation of each patient with respect to their physical condition in order to include them in the pool of telemonitored patients. Doctors have to make an assessment of risks and benefits with respect to inclusion in the pool of telemonitored patients. Not all patients can be included in telemonitoring. In general, those who have chronic diseases which require monitoring, or those who present occasional medical problems but are in good physical conditions, e.g., a young patient requiring a visit before a small surgical operation.

Several changes can also apply to tasks performed by healthcare staff (nurses) and administrative units[4] as it will be detailed in Chapter 3. For instance, there is a new task concerning the internal management of telemonitoring, reshuffling of shifts and formally including time frames and schedules to read and study collected parameters. Additionally, video consultation requires reorganizing appointments.

Moreover, a new task (which is perceived as temporary) concerns the digital transcription of a previous diagnosis and parameters of patients. At the current stage, the sector is still paper-abundant and there are also trade-offs perceived by doctors in using digital transcription, as it is seen as subtraction of time from visiting, curing, and treating. This has been particularly the case during the pandemic.

Focusing on caregivers and the provision of social assistance and support to patients in the use of monitoring devices, a new task emerges ensuring the proper application and use of remote monitoring devices. The caregiver plays a key role in facilitating the adoption of this process.

---

[4] The internal division between tasks performed by administrative profiles, nurses, assistants and in general health operators depends on the hierarchical structure of healthcare centers. Therefore, in some organizations it is likely that nurses are also in charge of more organizational type of activities such as arrangement of appointments.

The socio-health dimension is partly managed by healthcare facilities and private care systems. Social services handle the transition from the healthcare to the social dimension. However, social assistance is subsequently transferred to local councils, which may then contract cooperatives or private foundations to provide these services.

Overall, industry experts do not foresee deep transformation in tasks done by doctors but rather by administrative units which have the organizational burdens, and on caregivers which have the ultimate burden in terms of transmission and adaptation of technology.

The professional figures doing tele-visits are essentially the same and generically require the same competences of traditional medicine, but they are much more linked to the organizational structure. For example, if there is a delay in a televisit, it has to be communicated. At the end of the visit the recipe must be provided to patients. All these additional functions imply that the workload on the organizational part has increased.

Telemedicine does not substitute in-person visits. All activities done remotely have to be done in person if needed, meaning that the system has to be able to re-arrange the visit from remote to physical in case of emergency. Currently, the waiting list for tele-visits is the same as for in-person visits. The platforms used range from Skype to Teams and some other professionally tailored-made ones.

Indeed, as long as such technological devices facilitate timely diagnosis and somehow "automatic" diagnosis, that is, well before patients arrive to hospitals and regardless of the presence of a doctor onboard, this latter remains essential to ensure prompt (physical) intervention in critical situations. Therefore, in this specific context, substitution of nurses for doctors is not quite predictable. However, remote monitoring and, in case of emergency, all the activities carried out remotely highly impact on hospital organizational structures and work organization of hospital teams in the reference area implying several additional functions. For instance, if there is the need to re-arrange the schedule of surgery interventions due to an incoming patient requiring immediate rapid transfer into operating room.

In practice, low adoption is due to short sightedness of pay-back investment rules. Apart from cost amortization, barriers are very much due to the organizational dimension. Currently, telemedicine visits are unpaid in many public hospitals. This is not the case for private clinics that are imposing very costly access rates to tele-visits.

In terms of patient acceptance, while the use of wearables is often not well perceived, tele-visits are well received since they allow patients to have closer and more constant relationships with doctors and avoid the need for physical transfers. Further, medical devices must be compatible with the local health center, and therefore must be provided by it. However, there are problems with the integration of differentiated software used by hospitals, regional and local health agencies, private clinics and elderly residences.

Against this background, in the medium-long term telemonitoring should reduce hospital visits and emergency cases through continuous monitoring and prevention, therefore reducing the cost of hospital management. In this respect, Chapter 3 envisages major changes in the business model of healthcare centers concerning infrastructural investments, training of operators, and strengthening of administrative units.

1.4.3 Robots in Professional Cleaning

The sector presents some similarities at the intersection between logistics and healthcare. As the logistics segment is considered to perform low value-added phases, characterized by cascades of contractor and subcontractor procedures, in general short-lasting, it tends to rely on a cheap and abundant labor force, and it is clearly disconnected from technological producers. The actual distance with technological developers and the interface occurring only with dealers represent a major obstacle to develop tailor-made solutions which are required when a single service provider covers diverse final users as hospitals, stations, and warehouses.

On top of the obstacles related to the disintermediated value chain, there are a series of technical feasibility problems which need to be overcome before the adoption might become standardized. While the presence of dealers actually makes the acquisition easier by means of leasing contracts, the dealers are hardly able to meet the final client needs in terms of technical appropriateness and feasibility.

The use of professional cleaning robots faces a series of difficulties which can be attributed to the presence of highly unstructured workplaces to be cleaned which require fine, precise, agile and fast intervention relying on dexterity and fluid mobility. But there are also other relevant aspects such as the needs to operate in human-less environments: robots cannot be used in conjunction with densely populated spaces but can be largely used during night shifts since they are less likely to come in contact with humans. Moreover, there is an issue of delivery time of the service:

(currently available) professional cleaning robots require much more time with respect to human activity to clean the same square meter space.

At a more aggregate level, short-lasting contracts in the sector do not favor physical investments in such technologies (in case of subcontracting/outsourcing cleaning services to an outside company), and price-based competition discourages the use of cleaning robots in the sector.

If the COVID-19 pandemic has also pushed toward the substitution of humans with humanoid robots in this sector, some of the procedures and cleaning protocols required by the COVID-19 regulations have preferred the use of more traditional cleaning systems when compared to those based on the UVD robot which uses ultraviolet light to clean hospitals (Sostero, 2020).

Technological adoption is almost absent in cleaning activities; there are few exceptions concerning the development of in-house solutions (pilot phase), similarly, there are cases of "failed adoption", that is, the introduction of robots has subsequently been abandoned by companies performing cleaning activities due to the existence of several barriers. Obstacles to adoption are deep and diverse. They range from technical unfeasibility and lack of in-house technologically developed solutions. Cheap and abundant labor force performing labor-intensive activities relatively hard to automate inhibits technological, risky, investments. Barriers of adoption range from organizational/structural features (need of reconsidering the organization of spaces) to institutional elements (the inclusion of specific clauses in calls for tender). Key informants reveal that the participation to public tenders—which constitutes about 80–90% of total revenues of large companies working in the cleaning sectors—poses several constraints concerning the number of employees to be engaged. Furthermore, among the challenges of the adoption of professional cleaning robots, there is the need of adequate spaces and structures. So far in Italy there are few warehouses suitable for the implementation of these machines: new airports, universities, hospitals and shopping malls can be suitable for the application of cleaning robots but each structure needs to be carefully evaluated before planning their use. Overall, according to the interviewees layout of the places and specificities of the existing machines (i.e., Adlatus) do not permit their adoption; specifically, the navigation software of existing machines should be customized jointly by dealer/developer and client.

The interactions with key informants and contact persons of firms that have been engaged in the testing phase or adoption of professional cleaning robots have revealed a very rare use of these artifacts. In terms of the impact of adopted technology on occupational structure and task reconfiguration, companies perceive that the number of workers required to carry out cleaning tasks would not change immediately; they do not hypothesize in the short run any increases or decreases of employment due to the adoption of cleaning robots. In fact, institutional factors play a crucial role for companies offering cleaning services, while direct adoption by manufacturing firms or shopping malls appears to date a remote perspective. The outbreak of COVID-19 may have accelerated the adoption of cleaning robots in offices when employees are working from home.

Among the tasks affected by the introduction of these artifacts are those performed by cleaners, such as the supervision of the machine itself (in a specific time span). Moreover, tasks performed by administrative units of the company (operating in the cleaning sector) concerning the ability to elaborate a cost–benefit analysis on the use of the cleaning robot in a specific space (of the final user) or even deciding on the use of the machine in a specific case (inclusion of the specific service in a tender).

Against expectations of low degree of transformations, Chapter 4 highlights significant changes affecting cleaning workers, one of the most invisible categories, particularly in cases where machines have been introduced. In particular, the subjective dimension and the human agency traits of performing "dirty jobs" stand as characteristic elements of the Chapter.

1.5 Conclusions

This book is a research endeavor meant to shed new light on vulnerable workers, and the transformation of their working activity due to automation and digitalization. The book encompasses the findings of three industry studies in the service sector in Italy, and parallels with a benchmark case in the manufacturing sector, located in a peripheral country, Argentina. It advances a critical perspective on the technology-labor nexus, embracing several dimensions beyond the "economicistic" view, including human agency, workers' subjectivity, role of hierarchies, institutional bodies, and heterogeneity in firm capabilities.

The workplace analysis confirms the complexity in automating presumably low-value-added phases. According to the results of this book, human labor remains crucial in conducting activities that require the flexibility, adaptability and reconfiguration of physical tasks as in the case of cleaning. Even in sectors supposed to be highly automatable, such as in logistics, there exists "self-imposed limitations" on automation, responding to the flexibility requirement that AGV automation cannot ensure. In the health sector, automation intended as pure substitution for human activity has so far not been implemented: technologies more complementary rather than substitutive provide better support for the tasks performed by the medical staff.

Internal firm drivers play an important role across sectors. In the logistics segment, for instance, safety (and ergonomics), quality, productivity and reduction of low-value-added operations are crucial factors to evaluate the adoption and integration of AGVs. Cost-effectiveness may represent an important managerial driver in the cleaning sector: the potential removal of the operator driving the semi-automated cleaning machine during night shifts, paid more than a daily one, would have represented the saving of money.

Obstacles to automation are diverse, including technical infeasibility, which encompasses problems related to adapting AGV systems to plant layouts, the high level of rigidity in infrastructure organization, and the inadequacy of technologies available on the market.

Software obstacles matter since new technologies require a high level of integration: technologies can only be adopted if they are compatible with other existing technologies in use, and this limits the choice of adoption unless the decision is made to reconfigure the entire system. Market instability, institutional factors, and spatial and environmental constraints are other complementary factors influencing the drivers of adoption.

Drivers and barriers to technological adoption (except for institutional factors) are mainly linked to *techno-organizational capabilities* of the companies and their abilities to govern technological change. In addition, the low level of involvement of trade unions in the decisions concerning technological change is underscored in the Italian case studies. Unions are not recorded to intervene in the matter of technological innovation, and this is understood and confirmed by the trade unionists themselves when declaring that they "are managing the outcomes" of automation. The adoption of technological artifacts was, in all aspects, a managerial decision.

Elements of continuity and discontinuity with respect to manufacturing are underscored by this book. Continuity emerges in managerial decisions oriented to motives of productivity efficiency and cost saving/reduction of human intervention (in the case of AGVs). The most relevant driver of adoption remains the reduction of low-added-value phases and related low-added-value human functions/operators, in line with the just-in-time approach quite widespread in the manufacturing sector. In addition, the Argentinian case allows us to appreciate the relevance of strategic decisions taken by multinational corporations, and their relevance in affecting the direction of innovative strategies, together with the impact on the work process.

Discontinuity prevails in the lack of flexible adaptability of unstructured workplaces in being subject to automation. In particular, technical and institutional obstacles are such that widespread adoption of automation and monitoring technologies in services are still not the preferred choice.

Finally, while a task-based approach is useful for assessing the reconfiguration of work activities, occupations, and their hierarchical roles within organizations, remain crucial in shaping how technologies impact the world of work. Moreover, while initial concerns about the *future of work* primarily predicted workplaces without humans—where robots would replace human labor—it seems that, nowadays, such digital devices are increasingly making humans more robotic, with varying speeds across sectors. This trend of *robotization of humans* has already been recognized in the automotive sector and is emerging as a broader phenomenon affecting the entire world of work.

REFERENCES

Alvesson, M., & Karreman, D. (2011). *Qualitative research and theory development: Mystery as method*. Sage Publications.

Autor, D. H., Levy, F., & Murnane, R. J. (2003). The skill content of recent technological change: An empirical exploration. *The Quarterly Journal of Economics, 118*(4), 1279–1333. https://doi.org/10.1162/003355303322552801

Brynjolfsson, E., & McAfee, A. (2014). *The second machine age: Work, progress, and prosperity in a time of brilliant technologies*. W. W. Norton & Co.

Calvino, F., & Virgillito, M. E. (2018). The innovation employment nexus: A critical survey of theory and empirics. *Journal of Economic Surveys, 32*(1), 83–117. https://doi.org/10.1111/joes.12190

Cetrulo, A., Guarascio, D., & Virgillito, M. E. (2020). Anatomy of the Italian occupational structure: Concentrated power and distributed knowledge. *Industrial and Corporate Change, 29*(6), 1345–1379. https://doi.org/10.1093/icc/dtaa050

Cirillo, V., Evangelista, R., Guarascio, D., & Sostero, M. (2021a). Digitalization, routineness and employment: An exploration on Italian task-based data. *Research Policy, 50*(7), 104079. https://doi.org/10.1016/j.respol.2020.104079

Cirillo, V., Rinaldini, M., Staccioli, J., & Virgillito, M. E. (2021b). Technology vs. workers: The case of Italy's Industry 4.0 factories. *Structural Change and Economic Dynamics, 56*, 166–183. https://doi.org/10.1016/j.strueco.2020.09.007

Cirillo, V., Mina, A., & Ricci, A. (2024). Digital technologies, labor market flows and training: Evidence from Italian employer-employee data. *Technological Forecasting and Social Change, 209*, 123735. https://doi.org/10.1016/j.techfore.2024.123735

Eisenhardt, K. M. (1989). Building theories from case study research. *Academy of Management Review, 14*(4), 532–550. https://doi.org/10.5465/amr.1989.4308385

Fernández-Macías, E., & Bisello, M. (2022). A comprehensive taxonomy of tasks for assessing the impact of new technologies on work. *Social Indicators Research, 159*(2), 821–841. https://doi.org/10.1007/s11205-021-02768-7

Fernández-Macías, E., & Hurley, J. (2017). Routine-biased technical change and job polarization in Europe. *Socio-Economic Review, 15*(3), 563–585. https://doi.org/10.1093/ser/mww016

Ford, M. (2015). *The rise of the robots*. Basic Books.

Gutelius, B., & Theodore, N. (2019). *The future of warehouse work: Technological change in the U.S. logistics industry*, UC Berkeley Labor Center.

Hatton. (2017). Mechanisms of invisibility: Rethinking the concept of invisible work. *Work, Employment and Society, 31*(2), 336–351. https://doi.org/10.1177/0950017016674894

ISTAT. (2022). Rapporto Istat. Chapter 4: Le diverse forme della diseguaglianza, https://www.istat.it/storage/rapporto-annuale/2022/Rapporto_Annuale_2022.pdf

Kagermann, H., Wahlster, W., & Helbig, J. (2013). Recommendations for implementing the strategic initiative INDUSTRIE 4.0. Heilmeyer und Sernau, Germany.

Litwin, A. (2020). *Technological change in health care delivery: Its drivers and consequences for work & workers*. UC Berkeley Labor Center.

Montobbio, F., Staccioli, J., Virgillito, M. E., & Vivarelli, M. (2024). The empirics of technology, employment and occupations: Lessons learned and challenges ahead. *Journal of Economic Surveys, 38*(5), 1622–1655. https://doi.org/10.1111/joes.12601

Pfeiffer, S. (2014). Digital labour and the use-value of human work. On the importance of labouring capacity for understanding digital capitalism. *tripleC: Communication, Capitalism & Critique. Open Access Journal for a Global Sustainable Information Society, 12*(2), 599–619. https://doi.org/10.31269/triplec.v12i2.545

Pfeiffer, S. (2016). Robots, Industry 4.0 and humans, or why assembly work is more than routine work. *Societies, 6*(2), 16. https://doi.org/10.3390/soc6020016

Pfeiffer, S. (2018). The 'future of employment' on the shop floor: Why production jobs are less susceptible to computerization than assumed. *International Journal for Research in Vocational Education and Training, 5*(3), 208–225. https://doi.org/10.13152/IJRVET.5.3.4

Pfeiffer, S., & Suphan, A. (2015). The labouring capacity index: Living labouring capacity and experience as resources on the road to industry 4.0. Retrieved January, 30.

PwC. (2016). Shifting patterns. The future of the logistics industry. https://www.pwc.com/sg/en/publications/assets/future-ofthe-logistics-industry.pdf

PwC. (2020). Transport and logistics barometer. https://www.pwc.de/de/transport-und-logistik/transport-and-logistics-barometer-h1-2020.pdf

Sostero, M. (2020). Automation and robots in services: Review of data and taxonomy, JRC Working Papers Series on Labour, Education and Technology, No. 2020/14, European Commission, Joint Research Centre (JRC), Seville.

Staccioli, J., & Virgillito, M. E. (2021). The present, past, and future of labor-saving technologies. *Handbook of labor, human resources and population economics* (pp. 1–16). Springer International Publishing.

Wood, A. J. (2021). Algorithmic management consequences for work organisation and working conditions (No. 2021/07). JRC Working Papers Series on Labour, Education and Technology.

CHAPTER 2

Logistics Under Automation and Digitalisation: How Technology *Displaces* Human Work

Valeria Cirillo, Francesco S. Massimo, Matteo Rinaldini, and Jacopo Staccioli

Abstract Logistics operations, central to global capitalism, are transforming due to automation and digital technologies like Automatic Guided Vehicles (AGVs), especially in warehouses. Despite technological advances, the sector relies on a low-skilled workforce often facing

---

V. Cirillo
Department of Political Sciences, University of Bari 'Aldo Moro', Bari, Italy

F. S. Massimo (✉)
Sciences Po, Paris, France
e-mail: francescosabato.massimo@sciencespo.fr

University of Bologna, Bologna, Italy

M. Rinaldini
University of Modena and Reggio Emilia, Reggio Emilia, Italy

J. Staccioli
Catholic University of Milan, Milan, Italy

© The Author(s), under exclusive license to Springer Nature Switzerland AG 2025
V. Cirillo et al. (eds.), *Technology and Work in Services*,
https://doi.org/10.1007/978-3-031-88149-7_2

precarious conditions, including low wages, unsafe environments, and migrant worker exploitation. AGVs have not replaced human labour, as management values human flexibility over full automation to meet market demands, limiting AGV-driven job replacement. Rather, automation *displaces* labour, leading to work reorganisation. AGVs significantly reshape tasks, professional roles, and organisational boundaries. Their impact varies across companies, with technologically autonomous firms like Amazon experiencing deeper labour reorganisation and intensified value extraction. Automation's integration depends on corporate governance and market roles, creating uneven effects on workers.

Keywords Automated guided vehicles · Logistics · Task reconfiguration · Division of labour · Corporate strategies

2.1 Introduction

The logistics sector is central to the capitalist mode of production and to the global circulation of commodities. It has experienced a significant transformation due to the technological advancements and economic changes over the past decade, conventionally considered at the avant-garde of process automation, especially in the warehouse industry. Particularly noteworthy is its leadership in digital transformation, often accompanied by the integration of algorithmic management practices into everyday operations (Montobbio et al., 2022, 2024).

In addition to being exposed to significant technological changes, the logistics industry has a distinctive workforce composition. It is a global industry characterised primarily by a low-skilled workforce, offering predominantly low-quality jobs with unfavourable working conditions (Benvegnù et al., 2018; Bonacich & Wilson, 2011; Gutelius & Theodore, 2019; Newsome et al., 2013). This is evident in its relatively lower levels of employment protection compared to the manufacturing sector. Workers in this field often face hazardous conditions such as wage underpayment, dangerous working environments, and long working hours. Migrant workers, in particular, are at high risk of labour exploitation in this sector. Logistics management companies typically subcontract labour to employment agencies or rely on independent contractors, which further increases the potential for exploitation and the likelihood of deteriorating working conditions due to pressure on labour costs.

These two elements—being at the forefront of adopting automation technologies and primarily relying on low-skilled workers—make logistics a very interesting sector to examine when evaluating how the development of technologies is affecting labour and reshaping its organisation at the workplace level.

Therefore, following the tradition of industry studies (Hammerling, 2022), the objective of this chapter is to precisely examine how and why technological change is unfolding in logistics and assess what this change could mean for different groups of workers, with a special focus on low-skilled jobs, which, as mentioned, represent a significant portion of the entire labour pool employed.

In this chapter, we direct our attention further to a particular type of technology that is prevalent in warehouses: Automatic Guided Vehicles (AGVs). These vehicles demonstrate a remarkably high adoption rate and have reached an advanced stage of development. According to McKinsey (2023), AGVs should be classified as "the absolute minimum needed to remain competitive in the digital logistics technology race". They have often been portrayed as the quintessential technology poised to replace human labour, not only within logistics warehouses but also in other sectors like manufacturing. Hence, they serve as an ideal subject for an in-depth examination of the reorganisation of work associated with technological advancements.

AGVs can lead to changes in job roles and tasks for workers: while some may experience job displacement, others may need to adapt to new responsibilities related to the oversight, maintenance, or coordination of AGV operations.

Previous qualitative studies in the logistic industry, mainly referring to the US, have reported that automation has thus far not been associated with labour replacement as the activity is very labour-intensive; whereas AGVs have likely led to an intensification of work on top of labour-displacing effect. The tasks for which the impact of AGVs has generally been assessed include picking/stowing-type activities, inventory and quality check, handling and internal transportation.

Moreover, the integration of AGVs into workplace environments may also alter the physical work environment and workflows, potentially affecting factors such as workplace safety, ergonomic conditions, and the pace of work. Thus, while job displacement is a significant concern, the broader implications of technological change on working conditions, job roles, and occupational dynamics should also be carefully considered.

This chapter aims to provide new evidence based on a qualitative analysis from in-depth fieldwork conducted during 2021 and 2022 in three major logistics plants located in Italy: Philip Morris Manufacturing and Technology Bologna; Poste Italiane—Centro di Meccanizzazione Postale Bologna, and Amazon Fulfilment Center—Passo Corese.

Although these companies are all leaders in their respective markets—e-commerce, postal services, and tobacco/cigarette manufacturing—and have all introduced AGVs in their operations, they also exhibit significant differences. The latter arise not only from the variations in their final products or services but also from their diverse capacities to manage technological changes at the plant level and the varying degrees of governance established for these technologies by each company.

Drawing on previous empirical research based on the US (Gutelius & Theodore, 2019), we could expect that the application of AGVs even in the Italian logistics industry may lead to work intensification, linked to reduced autonomy of workers and simplification and fragmentation of tasks. However, these changes could not manifest uniformly across all logistic workplaces given the specificities of each plant, mainly concerning techno-organisational capabilities and strategic orientation towards technological adoption of the company. If this is the case, we should expect different degrees of machine integration in work processes reflected into a more or less intense *displacement* of human work.

To provide a preview of results, the qualitative analysis has revealed that the adoption of AGVs did not result in labour replacement, but rather in substantial labour displacement across the three plants. Moreover, concerning the impacts of automation technology on work activity (especially regarding control/self-latitude, tasks, and skills), the comparative study of labour processes highlighted that the impacts of AGVs on work activity vary across cases. In what follows, we detail these contributions.

The rest of the chapter is structured as follows: Sect. 2.1.1 provides a brief discussion on AGVs and their impact on work organisation and workers' skills. Sections 2.1.2–2.1.4 presents the qualitative research and the methodology applied. Sections 2.1.5 and 2.1.8 detail the results. Finally, Sect. 2.2 concludes the chapter.

2.1.1 Putting AGVs in Context

Over the past few decades, the logistics sector has undergone significant transformations due to technological advancements and economic restructuring at a global scale. The dissolution of traditional production processes and the rise of global value chains elevated logistics from a supportive role within companies to a standalone domain in business management, as already noted by Allen (1997) and Bonacich and Wilson (2011).

The effective management of inventory, just-in-time production, and transportation is pivotal for maintaining and enhancing a firm's competitive edge. Concurrently, the trend of manufacturing decentralisation has led to a paradoxical concentration of capital and centralised control in the logistics industry (Mourtzis & Doukas, 2012). This shift has been facilitated and necessitated by advancements in Information and Communication Technology (ICT) and escalating competition in delivery costs and timelines, marking a "logistics revolution" that impacts both the transportation and manufacturing sectors, significantly influencing corporate governance in logistics and supply chain management (Gupta et al., 2019).

More recently, the concept referred to as "Logistics 4.0" (Strandhagen et al., 2017) involves the utilisation of technologies such as artificial intelligence, blockchain, cloud computing, and the Internet of Things (IoT) to facilitate automation and planning. This extends from the execution of programmed tasks to a stage where functions are performed (at least partially) autonomously, and information is exchanged within a cross-organisational framework of cyber-physical processes (Klumpp & Zijm, 2019; Sigov et al., 2022).

In this scenario, major changes occurred both at the level of internal logistics, which encompasses in-house transportation and storage, and third-party logistics (3PL) providers that offer specialised logistics services to businesses, covering both B2B and B2C models.

According to the extensive fieldwork performed by Gutelius and Theodore (2019) in the US, there is a clear effort in reducing labour costs at the core of the logistic industry predominantly through lower wages. Therefore, besides technological advancements, technological adoption has so far been primarily directed towards the introduction of monitoring devices and digital technologies, which enable standardising and de-skilling some portions of working activity, rather than pure automation. Wearables used by operators and sensors, or RFID tags applied to goods, are the current state of the art. On top of that, algorithmic management software is used to track the production flow and monitor workers' performance.

In this panorama, the adoption of AGVs is part of a large technological overhaul in logistics, involving a suite of interconnected technologies. Presently, a range of warehousing technologies, such as real-time distribution centre performance management, AGV-based goods-to-person systems, and warehouse management systems, have already been widely adopted or are approaching widespread use. Digital warehouse twins, dynamic labour management, and gesture and motion tracking have been included in pilot programs, while fully automated item picking, network digital twins, and smart shelves are still at an infant stage.

Concerning the impact on work, previous contributions have emphasised, on the one hand, the increasing needs of specific skills to properly interact with the new machines especially for low-skill workers, and on the other hand, the risks of jobs displacement related to the introduction of digital and automation technologies in logistics.

Regarding the first aspect, some studies building on a functionalist approach have primarily focused on the increasing need for specific skills and competencies to interact with new machines. These studies, which are mainly based on interviews with warehouse managers, human resources officers, quality managers, and logistics project managers, have identified a set of digital skills deemed "strategic" for workers in the sector. These skills range from "coordinating actions with automated handling, storage, palletization systems" to "performing first-level maintenance on connected objects commonly found in warehouses", "managing and optimizing flows using digital interfaces" or "communicating as well as positioning oneself in digital and virtual environments" (Hocquelet, 2020; Koh & Yuen, 2022). All in all, these studies view digital skills as proficiency in using a range of technologies or "tools".

However, a notable limitation of this emphasis on the abstract measurement and categorisation of skills is the lack of attention to the complexity of skills required in actual workplace contexts. Moreover, it is crucial to consider digital skills within the context of work processes and their connections to broader knowledge that may influence how these skills are applied and acquired.

On this line, a more critical perspective suggests that digital skills do not solely result from technology (Edwards & Ramirez, 2016). For example, a new robot may have a pre-programmed procedure or menu that varies in complexity, reflecting what Thompson and Laaser (2021) describe as "first-order choices" in technology design, made prior to its adoption in the workplace. However, decisions still need to be made regarding which technology to acquire, whether a robot integrates with other digital systems, whether its full capabilities are utilised, and how tasks and skills are redistributed among different groups of workers. From this perspective, earlier qualitative examinations based on the logistic industry have underscored that while automation via AGVs and similar technologies has not resulted in a straightforward substitution of labour, primarily due to the labour-intensive nature of the logistics domain, it has indeed led to a heightened intensity of work and reshaped the characteristics of specific tasks suggesting a new division of labour between logistic operators and machines.

The influence of AGVs is particularly evident in activities like picking, inventory verification, and internal transportation. Moreover, their integration within logistics is perceived as a potential avenue to increase the intensity of labour while diminishing worker autonomy, as well as streamlining and fragmenting tasks. In this discussion, several empirical works have focused on specific cases such as Walmart (Appelbaum & Lichtenstein, 2006; Brunn, 2006; Lichtenstein, 2009; Petrovic & Hamilton, 2006) and Amazon (Allison & Reese, 2023; Alimahomed-Wilson et al., 2020; Barthel & Rottenbach, 2017; Delfanti, 2021; Kassem, 2023; Lee et al., 2024; Massimo, 2020, 2024).

Lots of contributions in this tradition mainly related to the *Labour Process Theory* focused on case studies that underplayed the structural constraints and the economic dynamics shaping the design, development and deployment of technology (Braverman, 1974; Burawoy, 1978; Knights & Willmott, 1990; Boreham et al, 2008; Thompson & Laaser, 2021).

In this chapter, we take a step forward by studying the organisation of work under automation in three leading companies—Philip Morris Manufacturing and Technology; Poste Italiane; Amazon Fulfillment Center—that occupy different positions in the global governance of digital technologies. This allows us to gain a sort of "macro" perspective on the dynamics behind technologies that are usually absent in most workplace analyses. Although these three companies hold monopolistic positions in their respective markets, they differ in terms of the generation, ownership, and control of technology. This defines some of them as being in a position of "dependency" and others as having "global leadership", which translates into the firm's capacity to control and adapt the integration of technology within its internal organisational environment. When evaluating the consequences in terms of work, this distinction is particularly important for understanding the scope of management actions and highlighting the negotiating spaces available to workers and their representatives.

2.1.2 A Workplace Analysis: Case Selection and Fieldwork

This chapter builds on a qualitative analysis derived from extensive fieldwork conducted in Italy during 2021 and 2022 as part of the research project "Case Studies of Automation in Services". More in detail the research comprised two distinct phases: case selection and fieldwork.

2.1.3 Case Selection Strategy: Three Different Cases of AGVs Adoption

In the initial phase, a shortlist of potential case studies was identified through informal interviews and interactions with representatives and key informants from various companies. Exploratory interviews were conducted to gather information on the diffusion of digital technologies, and particularly, AGVs in logistics, focussing on their macro-impacts on economic and industrial processes. Three establishments were selected accordingly:

- Philip Morris Manufacturing and Technology Bologna (Philip Morris MT-B) manufactures no-smoke tobacco sticks. Philip Morris MT-B is a manufacturing plant dedicated to the prototyping and producing production of tobacco sticks meant to be heated with a heat control device rather than burned like cigarettes, but logistics operations have become crucial with the introduction of AGVs, since automatic vehicles allow the physical and digital connection of the different departments. The site is a "greenfield" plant, funded ex novo in 2016 as a pilot site for the manufacturing of this new product, and it is involved in raw material transformation and product assembly. The plant receives raw tobacco from suppliers and other raw materials for the fabrication of filters and special paper for the wrapping. A dock area is dedicated to the packaging of tobacco sticks and shipment to national and international markets, while an automatised internal warehouse (High Bay Warehouse) and another external warehouse are stocked with raw materials and finished and packed products. The internal logistics department is outsourced to a Spanish provider, Logista, which employs around 270 units at the plant.

- Poste Italiane—Centro di Meccanizzazione Postale Bologna (Poste Italiane CMP-B) is a primary logistics sorting facility of the Italian national postal service. The plant employs around 700 workers. The site was established in 1995 and is one of the 23 CMPs operated by Poste Italiane in the country. CMPs are the core of the country's postal distribution network. The operations carried out by CMPs are the receipt of mail coming from post box and postal offices; registration, regrouping, sorting; and lastly the shipment of treated mail depending on the destinations within the sphere of CMPs' competence.
- Amazon Fulfillment Center—Passo Corese (Amazon FC-PC) is a greenfield warehouse where stowing, picking, checking, labelling and packing of online retail orders take place; the facility employs around 2000 workers. The site is run by a subsidiary of Amazon.com Inc., Amazon Italian Logistics S.r.l., which oversees the management of all Fulfillment Centers established in Italy. A Fulfillment Center is the main knot in the Amazon logistics network: a large warehouse in which e-commerce products are received, stored ("stowed") and prepared for shipment, i.e. picked, packed and loaded onto trucks. Fulfillment Centers store and process three kinds of items: (i) items owned, sold and shipped by Amazon; (ii) items owned by third-party sellers, sold on Amazon website and shipped by Amazon logistics services; (iii) items owned by third-party sellers, sold on third-party websites but shipped through Amazon logistics services. This multi-channel strategy turns Amazon into a platform for e-commerce and logistics services, as well as for data collection.

All three establishments have implemented digital software and hardware solutions, such as WMSs (Warehouse Management Systems) and AGVs

(Automated Guided Vehicles). However, they display significant differences in terms of development, governance, use, and maintenance of technologies (Cirillo et al., 2023). More in detail:

- In Philip Morris MT-B, AGVs were manufactured and provided by Oceaneering International, Inc. corporation, an overseas engineering and applied technology company based in Texas, USA. Currently, 34 AGVs operate at the plant. They are laser-guided and their main area of operation is the warehouse, where raw materials are loaded onto carts by Logista workers, the "spine" of a long corridor which connects the Primary and Secondary department and the shipment bays.
- In Poste Italiane CMP-B, the introduction of AGVs was planned in 2016 when Poste Italiane together with the Italy-based company Scaglia-Indeva developed the introduction of robots to carry out internal trolley movements. The provider designed and manufactured four AGVs with magnetic markers specifically for the CMP pilot plant in Bologna, which had been operating without AGVs for a long time—almost 30 years. Two years later, in 2018, Poste Italiane decided to extend the solution nationwide, adding a total of 60 Indeva AGVs to 10 CMPs across Italy. The investment was about €1.9 million. In the CMP-B, a total of 8 AGVs were introduced in 2018. By then, AGVs are used for automatic handling of objects and towing of trolleys (6-wheel trolleys, Pally and Lid and Roll containers).
- In Amazon FC-PC, AGVs were provided by Amazon Robotics, Amazon's division for research and the manufacturing of mobile robotic fulfilment systems. Amazon Robotics is the former Kiva System, a Massachusetts-based company that Amazon acquired in 2012 specifically for developing in-house robotics technology for its fulfillment centres.

2.1.4 *The Execution of the Fieldwork*

The second phase of our endeavour involved on-site visits to the selected establishments and conducting semi-structured interviews with various professionals including HR management, trade union representatives, technology specialists, and workers in key occupations affected by digital technologies. The interview template, designed to ensure comparability across establishments, focused on three main areas: the economic impact of the technology, its influence on work organisation, and its effects on tasks and job quality. This comprehensive approach aimed to provide insights into the broader implications of technology adoption within organisational contexts.

The fieldwork, conducted between 2021 and early 2022, faced challenges due to the Covid-19 pandemic restrictions. The audio of 22 interviews (see Table 2.4), each lasting approximately 45 minutes, was recorded and subsequently transcribed. A content analysis methodology was undertaken to systematically scrutinise each interview, focussing on several key dimensions, including the impact on work organisation, workflows, and processes within the studied companies. Additionally, attention was devoted to assessing the effects on employment patterns and working conditions resulting from the implementation of new technologies. Another crucial aspect analysed was the influence on the occupational composition, job profiles, and task content within the organisations. By thoroughly coding and analysing the interview transcripts, the research sought to provide insights into the multifaceted impacts of technological integration in the workplace, shedding light on changes in organisational dynamics, employment structures, and the overall work environment.

2.1.5 Results from Qualitative Analyses

In what follows, we present the main evidence stemming from the fieldwork and illustrate the findings according to three major dimensions: (i) deployment and integration of AGVs at the shop floor level; (ii) work organisation, categorised as replacement versus displacement of work; and (iii) work activity, encompassing control/self-latitude, tasks, and skills.

2.1.6 Deployment and Integration of AGVs at the Shopfloor Level: Three Different Cases of Technological Dependence

In contemporary capitalism, corporations vary in their internal innovation strategies or regimes, which primarily involve how technology is generated, developed, and integrated into the production process. As a result, some companies invest in research and development (R&D) with dedicated laboratories, while others rely on external technology markets or adhere to technological standards dictated by their specific value chain.

This also applies to the companies involved in this fieldwork. For example, Amazon and Philip Morris demonstrate high innovation capacity through patents, indicative of potential independence in technological use and development. In contrast, Poste Italiane exhibits lower patenting activity and potentially a higher level of technological dependence (Cirillo et al., 2023).

More in detail, a high level of technological dependence, combined with a low level of integration of the technology in the work process has been observed at Poste Italiane CMP-B, where the introduction of AGVs did not require any special reorganisation of the workflow. At Poste Italiane, AGVs are managed via a software program which was bought from the provider and is now owned by Poste Italiane. The software is controlled from the corporate headquarters, as well as on-site. However, AGVs are not digitally integrated with the remaining technological infrastructure, although they are linked to Poste Italiane's IT offices at headquarters. AGVs accomplish both general and auxiliary functions in relation to the rest of the processes and machinery.

- The general use of AGVs implies that every workstation and every machine can be served by AGVs. Every worker is trained to use them. However, given the relatively reduced number of units and the low degree of digital integration, their role remains auxiliary in relation to the global workflow.

A low level of dependence (centralisation of control in the use of the technology) is found at Philip Morris MT-B, despite a high fragmentation of the different actors dealing with the technology. This is obtained through a complex multi-layered governance (internal outsourcing). Philip Morris MT-B team does not run the AGVs directly: the running and maintenance of this technology is subcontracted to a local service provider, Simic Automation, with 28 employees at the plant. The basic logistic operations of warehousing, preparation, handling, loading, and unloading AGVs are outsourced to a subcontracted logistics services company, Logista, a Spain-based multinational group, which employs 270 workers at the plant, located in the shipment and warehousing areas. This multi-layered structure generates a complex system of governance for the production process and the AGVs which are remotely managed by Oceaneering International, Inc. who also provides a control system called SuperFROG®.

Philip Morris MT-B IT teams then integrate this software with an iMEL LES-MES (Logistic and Manufacturing Execution System).

- AGVs serve most workstations, and workers are trained to handle them according to their specific tasks. AGVs primarily support core production activities related to the production of tobacco sticks. AGVs' governance system shows a high degree of integration both in terms of hardware (AGVs intervene in many production phases) and software (AGVs are connected to the plant's central information system in real time).

A low level of dependence and a high level of integration (centralisation) were found also at Amazon FC-PC, even if centralisation is achieved through vertical integration rather than the internal outsourcing model that we found at Philip Morris MT-B. In contrast to Philip Morris MT-B, Amazon runs dozens of warehouses of this kind in Italy and the rest of the world, implying a certain level of standardisation and coordination. Amazon AGVs move shelves (called pods) allowing for faster stowing and picking. As said, AGVs are provided by Amazon Robotics, a Massachusetts-based company that Amazon acquired in 2012 specifically for developing in-house robotics technology for its fulfillment centers. Thus, unlike the other two cases, Amazon FC-PC is one of few companies able to develop AGV technology in-house. In terms of control and information governance, AGVs' movements are fully centralised. A unique WMS connects each AGV to a server, in order to have real-time transmission of registered orders and inventory updates. This system governs the entire Amazon network in Europe and enables standardised and synchronous storage management. This technology is provided by Amazon's IT division and servers are hosted by Amazon Web Services (AWS).

- Amazon AGVs are a typical example of fully internalised introduction and management of automation technology. Amazon's AGVs play a key role both from an organisational and spatial viewpoint, since they move the storage units located at the centre of each floor to a preferred area. Differently from Poste Italiane CMP-B, their role is not simply auxiliary, since they allow all operations related to storage and picking processes. However, they also have limited use since access is reserved to few professional figures such as pickers, stowers and the maintenance/troubleshooting team.

As shown in Table 2.1, while Philip Morris MT-B, a global leader in tobacco and cigarette production, has partially outsourced the management of AGVs, it still maintains control over the technology's deployment at the workshop level. In contrast, Poste Italiane, the public provider of mail services within Italy, has acquired the technology from an external provider without integrating it with its existing technological infrastructure. Amazon designed and implemented the technology of interest in-house through Amazon Robotics.

2.1.7 Work Organisation: Replacement/Displacement Dynamics

According to different levels of integration of technologies in the production process, we should expect heterogeneous forms of work reorganisation. Overall, it emerges that in all three plants there was no evidence of direct substitutions and expulsions of the workforce as a consequence of the introduction of AGVs. Actually, this first important result is in line with a large body of literature on this topic that suggests caution in considering the labour force substitution effects due to new technologies (Autor, 2015; Benanav, 2020; Carbonell, 2022; Cirillo et al., 2021).

However, there are contingent reasons, resulting from our case studies. Indeed, two of them (Philip Morris MT-B and Amazon FC-PC) are greenfield plants, so it was impossible to assess directly any impact on employment. On this basis, the plant management interviewed could deny any serious impact of the technology on employment. Quite the contrary, management claimed that, without the new technology, the opening of the new plant would have not been viable, resulting in a potential loss of investment and employment for the area. At Poste Italiane CMP-B, where the technology was introduced in quite an old plant, there was no net job loss. Additionally, the trade unions that were well-established within the workplace and the company supported the plan without significant concerns. In fact, they backed the restructuring without making any special demands, anticipating an improvement in working conditions, even while acknowledging the potential for a net reduction in employment.

Table 2.1 Automated guided vehicles in the three companies

Philip Morris Manufacturing and Technology Bologna	Poste Italiane—Centro di Meccanizzazione Postale Bologna	Amazon Fulfillment Center—Passo Corese
(i) Sophisticated governance system for both the production process and AGVs (ii) Plant layout and production processes are intentionally devised to accommodate AGVs from the site's conceptualisation: 34 AGVs are operational at the plant, interconnected via Wi-Fi and guided by lasers (iii) AGVs handle 80% of the transport operations within the plant, 20% of transport operations are manually conducted using forklifts by Logista operators (iv) Oceaneering International provides the SuperFROG AGV control system; the Philip Morris MT-B IT teams oversee the integration of this software with an IMEL LES-MES (logistic and manufacturing executive system)	(i) AGVs operate through a software program purchased from the provider and are now owned by Poste Italiane, as well as centrally controlled at the national level and also at the on-site level (ii) AGVs not digitally integrated with the broader technological infrastructure; instead, they are linked to POSTE's IT offices at the headquarters	(i) AGVs supplied by Amazon Robotics, formerly Kiva System, acquired by Amazon in 2012 to develop in-house robotic technology for its Fulfillment Centers, one of the few companies with in-house AGV development capabilities (ii) Warehouse Management System (WMS) connects individual AGVs to Amazon's website, ensuring real-time transmission of registered orders and inventory updates governing the entire Amazon network in Europe; it is a standardised and synchronous storage management

Let's say that [the adoption of AGVs] was welcomed, I would say, by all the trade unions. I remember a famous national meeting, I remember the national secretaries also seemed dazzled by what [the new technology] was … When a company invests in technology, there is a risk of a downturn in employment. But right from the start we had a different perception, like it's a technology that can help improve safety workload points, and it's a technology that's not so far-reaching that we'll lose jobs. That was the perception we had. After 3 years, I feel I can say that it has been confirmed. It is true that with a certain type of work we may have three [employees] instead of five, but the other two who no longer work at that workstation will not only allow their co-workers to rotate more on the workstations considered to be a bit heavier, but also take care of other types of work where we perhaps previously had difficulty, purely manual work...

POSTE-7 [Poste Italiane CMP-B, Trade Union Representative]

Although AGVs have not directly affected the levels of employment, we found important and structural changes on the organisation of work and the reconfiguration of tasks (Table 2.2). Rather than a mere replacement, automation technologies led to an important displacement of jobs, tasks and skills. For instance, both at Poste Italiane CMP-B and Philip Morris MT-B, AGVs replaced most of the forklift drivers, whose tasks were reallocated between machines and workers. At Amazon FC-PC, such a replacement did not take place for the simple reason that forklift drivers were already marginal in the previous model of work organisation.

2.1.8 Work Activity: Control and Self-Latitude of Work

Although the introduction of AGVs did not lead to a general reduction in the number of employees, changes in tasks have been observed. More in detail, the introduction of AGVs in Poste Italiane CMP-B did not require any special reorganisation of the workflow, but some changes in terms of tasks have been registered. According to interviewees (especially managers and union officials), a reduction of tasks involving manual handling of heavy loads occurred. However, comparing these statements to those of some operators, a more nuanced picture is needed. In fact, operators pointed to the persistence of some heavy physical tasks even after the introduction of AGVs. While it is true that AGVs can now move heavy loads from one part of the warehouse to another, the final manoeuvre of adjusting the cart's position around the workstation must be manually performed by the operator. For what concerns more qualified tasks of interaction with the robot (e.g. troubleshooting), clear boundaries were drawn. In the case of minor troubles, POSTE operators can operate on the AGVs with simple maintenance operations (all operators are authorised to provide such initial intervention). However, in case the problem persists, operators must call the technical team. The latter consists of

Table 2.2 Labour process restructuring in relation to AGVs

Philip Morris Manufacturing and Technology Bologna	Poste Italiane—Centro di Meccanizzazione Postale Bologna	Amazon Fulfillment Center—Passo Corese
New groups of professional figures were created for the management of AGVs (i) the technical and maintenance worker who monitors the AGVs on the ground and from the control room (ii) the Logistics Automation team at PMI also monitoring the AGVs and the performance of SIMIC at a higher level (iii) the execution of specific manual tasks before in the hand of forklift drivers has now been outsourced to an external company, named Logista	AGVs at POSTE ITALIANE operate as an "auxiliary" technology whose introduction did not massively affect the organisation of work and the tasks of workers Before the introduction of AGVs, when POSTE workers needed to transport sorted mail to another area, they called forklift operators or even transported carts on their own After the introduction of AGVs, workers can now use AGVs instead of moving their own carts or calling for a forklift driver • Not requiring any specific reorganisation of the labour process; • Introduction of AGVs has not resulted in a general decline in employment; certain jobs, however, such as forklift drivers, have experienced a decrease following the implementation of AGVs	AGVs contribute to the reshuffling of the pick and stow tasks, leading to the introduction of new jobs, such as that of Amnesty Responder or that for technical robotics maintenance, but their introduction did not lead to the disappearance of forklifts

Poste Italiane specialised operators and supervisors, along with specialists employed by external companies. Members of the technical team also train Poste Italiane CMP-B operators on the matter. Overall, it seems that operators experienced a slight increase in informational tasks (basic troubleshooting) but also in physical tasks (manually adjusting the cart to the workstation).

If there's a problem with the AGVs, we usually handle it ourselves—we know the machine well by now. If there is a problem that is technical, we have a phone number that we call and tell them the problem.

POSTE-7 [Mail Sorter/AGV Operator]

At Philip Morris MT-B forklift operators have largely been replaced by AGVs, and new company functions (and job profiles) have been established to govern AGVs and their logistics automation and maintenance. As detailed in Table 2.2, there are four main categories of operators interacting with AGVs: (a) logistics operators (employed by Logista), who carry out loading and unloading activities in the logistics areas of the plant; (b) technical-maintenance operators (employed by Simic), who monitor the activities of AGVs and intervene to solve operational problems; (c) logistics automation supervisors (employed by Philip Morris MT-B), who monitor the performance of AGVs and Simic's technical-maintenance operators at a higher level; (d) production operators (employed by Philip Morris MT-B), who receive raw materials and semi-finished products via AGVs. Besides them, there are production operators (the largest group of workers in the plant), in charge of assembling the different components of the final product. Tasks and jobs are not affected in the same way by AGVs. Logistics operators (employed by Logista) continue to perform simple manual tasks for which no special skills are required. However, the use of AGVs has changed some loading and unloading operations. More importantly, logistics operators also have to solve some basic problems that can occur with AGVs during work time. It is no coincidence that the management insists on improving the digital skills of logistics operators.

> What has really changed is that the transport is no longer manual but automatic, so the activity that the operator used to carry on was to take a pallet, prepare it so that the forklifts can pass through and go up ... They still do it. The only thing that is a plus is that they had to increase their capabilities. Because in order to prepare a material, they not only have to do physical activity but also have to understand how to manage a system so that the pallet is picked up. [...] The need for the vehicle to have a compliant load required a certain awareness in preparing the loads in a certain way and to be able to do basic troubleshooting. So it's a small change, but it makes the operator feel the need to work better in order to have a better service, because the operators are very aware of the

fact that if they leave a vehicle stationary and do not intervene, etc.—the factory being huge—we cannot wait for the Simic support to arrive and decipher the problem. They can already operate alone because they have an initial level of intervention. Understandably, in front of some classes of problems they cannot intervene. For the classes that require an adjustment of the load or removal of the obstacle and a single reset, they can do it by themselves, so let's say that it is a small change, but for them in terms of capability, however, they are trained, so they have some extra elements.

PMMTB-1 [PMI Supervisor for Logistics Automation]

The Simic team mainly consists of professionals with technical education, while the supervising Philip Morris MT-B team is composed of engineers. The latter remain in the control room, from where they can monitor the operations of the AGVs and intervene in case of major malfunction. As for production operators, the introduction of AGVs has simplified and eliminated a wide range of mainly physical activities. Among them, loading and unloading of material. At the same time, these operators are trained in the use of AGVs and can order a supply of material using a software tool (iMEL LES-MES). In general, the introduction of AGVs has standardised work activities by reducing work time spent in low value-added and non-core activities. At the same time, physical tasks were significantly reduced and social interactions with colleagues in logistics areas decreased.

When considering Amazon FC-PC, it is challenging to assess the impact of AGVs on work, as there was no prior situation for comparison. However, we could compare it to the traditional pick and stow process used in previous-generation warehouses. Additionally, another comparison is possible within the site, as a traditional operation known as "pallet picking" is still conducted in a small section of the plant. Compared to Poste Italiane CMP-B, and even Philip Morris MT-B (where AGVs remain assigned to an auxiliary manufacturing function), AGVs at Amazon FC-PC are associated with deep changes in the organisation of work. Compared to legacy warehouses, work activities of pickers and stowers have been reshuffled entirely, and new professional figures have been introduced.

In terms of task reconfiguration, AGVs contribute to the overhaul of the pick and stow, leading to the introduction of new jobs, such as the Amnesty Responder (maintenance operator) or technical robotics maintenance (see Table 2.2). Anyway, Amazon FC-PC AGVs did not replace most of the forklifts, as happened at Poste Italiane CMP-B and Philip

Morris MT-B, because these positions were already marginal when the warehouse was built. AGVs move PODs (the storage units) between pick and stow workstations across the floor. Differently from Poste Italiane CMP-B and Philip Morris MT-B where, with greater leeway, operators call the AGVs when they need items and components, at Amazon FC-PC pickers and stowers do not control the movements of the AGVs, which are centrally managed by the Warehouse Management System. When the single operation of pick or stow is completed (i.e. the item is retrieved or stored in the shelf and registered through a series of informational input), the AGV moves the pod away to another workstation. Overall, the introduction of AGVs expands the tendency of job de-skilling. Stow, pick, and pack work—i.e. the vast majority of the jobs—becomes increasingly similar in terms of tasks. The boundaries between these occupations are so blurred, that management does not provide specific job descriptions. Such a configuration allows greater internal flexibility and grants management with discretionary control over the allocation of workers on tasks:

> For us, the [unique] role is that of the warehouse operator. Given the low level of complexity of each of these tasks, there is no particular requirement associated with the indication of a job description because the autonomy is really low in relation to the decision-making possibility. Really low, because the whole process is absolutely guided step by step for the operator and then makes it really simple, so we do not have precise job descriptions. [...] For us, [workers] are all "Associates" and they are all to be, like, say, using contractual terminology, Warehouse Operators. Regardless of the process, of the task that they accomplish. That is, we try to make everyone know how to do all the processes, right? To facilitate job rotation among people, but there's no constraint like "I know two processes so I should do them".

AMAZON-7 [Amazon Plant HR Manager]

As said, the Amnesty Responder is a new position introduced for troubleshooting on the robotic floor, which is a fenced area off limits to human operators. Only specific jobs have authorised access, and only for maintenance tasks. The Amnesty Responder intervenes when one or more AGVs stop—this human intervention is allowed when an item falls down from the storage unit to the floor. The AGV sensor detects an obstacle in its path and stops, emitting an alarm. The Amnesty Responder receives the alert on a digital tool (usually a tablet), enters the floor, certifies the problem and attempts to fix it according to standard procedures. Sometimes the problem is more complicated, and the maintenance team is expected to intervene. In any case, operators entering the robotic floor are equipped with a special vest which projects a magnetic cone detected by the AGVs (Table 2.3).

Table 2.3 Task reconfiguration in relation to AGVs

Philip Morris Manufacturing and Technology Bologna	Poste Italiane—Centro di Meccanizzazione Postale Bologna	Amazon Fulfillment Center—Passo Corese
(i) Impact of AGVs varies across tasks and roles: – Logista operators continue simple manual tasks without specialised skills, but AGVs have altered some loading and unloading operations; enhancement of digital skills – Production operators have experienced a simplification and elimination of various physical activities, including material loading and unloading; standardised and streamlined work activities have reduced low-value-added and non-core tasks, saturating working time; physical tasks have significantly decreased, leading to a decline in social interactions among colleagues in logistics areas	(i) POSTE operators are authorised to intervene with simple maintenance operations, and all operators can perform these initial interventions (ii) Slight increase in informational tasks (basic troubleshooting) as well as in physical tasks (manually adjusting the cart to the workstation) (iii) Autonomy to decide among themselves who can use the AGV for a specific operation, horizontal coordination without direct intervention from a supervisor	(i) Limited autonomy and highly standardised tasks at Amazon operators having no choice in AGV use, except for the Amnesty Responder and maintenance team

To sum up, the three cases studied represent examples of low (Poste Italiane CMP-B), medium (Philip Morris MT-B), and high (Amazon FC-PC) impact of AGVs on tasks and jobs. This qualitative difference is also reflected in the quantitative use of AGVs (10 in Poste Italiane CMP-B, 34 in Philip Morris MT-B, dozens in Amazon FC-PC). AGVs bring different degrees of task and job reconfiguration. The impact appears higher at Amazon FC-PC, where AGVs directly affect the tasks of most operators. At Philip Morris MT-B, the direct impact appears less pronounced but still detectable. At Poste Italiane CMP-B, this was even less pronounced.

Moreover, the effect of the introduction of AGVs on tasks and skills is also different in qualitative terms. At Poste Italiane CMP-B we found evidence of a slight increase in informational tasks, even if this increase is less significant for low-rank operators, who also report an increase in physical tasks. At Philip Morris MT-B, the increase in digital tasks is also common to all groups of workers, even with more intensity for the higher ranks; finally, at Amazon FC-PC, low-rank operators (the vast majority of the workforce) experienced no remarkable increase of digital tasks despite Amazon FC-PC is the case where the introduction of robotic technology has been by far the most pervasive.

Based on this evidence, we can assess that POSTE exhibits the highest degree of technological subordination and a relatively less pronounced impact on the reconfiguration of labour division. In contrast, Amazon demonstrates the highest level of technological independence and in-factory integration, alongside a reinforcement of the division of labour. Positioned between these two, Philip Morris MT-B, with its sophisticated technological governance, shows a hierarchical reconfiguration of the division of labour at the shop floor level.

2.2 Conclusions

The circulation of goods and services across the globe is a central feature of capitalist societies and the logistics sector, organising these exchanges, is the privileged arena for experimenting with the digital and automated technologies potentially accelerating these transactions. Within the sector, heterogeneous corporations operate with different degrees of autonomy with respect to the technologies in place. Some of them have the capabilities—both technological and organisational—to "govern" the technologies in use; others simply adapt to the technological standards of the value chains in which they participate. This should be kept in mind when assessing the relationship between technologies, work and vulnerable workers. The qualitative analysis underlying this article emphasised three main points.

First, differently from what is conventionally believed, labour replacement by means of automation technologies has not yet occurred. Instead, different dynamics of displacement are taking place, although not pervasively (e.g. forklift drivers have decreased but not disappeared). The explanation of this partial displacement is the preference of management to ensure redundancy and respond to the market requirement of flexibility that AGV automation is not able to guarantee. Meaning that human labour remains crucial in conducting activities that require flexibility and adaptability.

Second, the limited impact of automation on employment does not prevent AGVs from deeply affecting work organisation. Tasks and organisational reconfiguration appear to be the most significant changes, with considerable effects on professional and departmental boundaries.

Third, automation technologies such as AGVs have proven to re-organise work in the logistics sector, and this varies across plants according to the level of dependence/autonomy of each company regarding the adopted technology. More specifically and surprisingly, the deepest reorganisation of work has occurred in those corporations where there is a higher level of technological autonomy, such as in the case of Amazon. The greater the integration of technology into the work process, the more profound the extraction of value from labour, which is not replaced but displaced to guarantee enough flexibility.

Finally, although a task-based approach can be useful in assessing the reconfiguration of the working activities, occupations and their hierarchical roles inside the organisation remain a crucial aspect in affecting the unfolding of technologies upon the world of work as the distribution of skills across groups of workers clearly demonstrated in the Philip Morris case.

Of course, this study has several limitations. The focus on the workplace should not overlook the global context in which companies operate. From this perspective, the analysis has not sufficiently addressed cross-country differences, as all three workplaces under examination are located in Italy. Additionally, it would be beneficial to examine a wider range of technological artefacts and to enrich the analysis by considering multiple points in time.

Despite these limitations, the study sheds light on a usually neglected dimension: the deployment and integration of technology at the shop floor level, which reflects varying degrees of corporate power on a global scale, and its interaction with labour process restructuring. This aspect is likely to influence how vulnerable workers are impacted on their work processes and their ability to negotiate and shape technological changes. Unfortunately, we were unable to fully explore this aspect due to the low participation of trade unions and delegates in the interviews. Including this dimension in future investigations remains essential, given the strategic role of the logistics sector within global capitalism.

Appendix

See Table 2.4.

Table 2.4 Distribution of interviews by company

Company	Interview code	Occupational title	Sex	Main task	Company Seniority (year of beginning)	Contract
Amazon	AMAZON-1	Worker 1	F	Pick/Stow	2017	Permanent
	AMAZON-2	Worker 2	F	Pick/Stow	2020	Permanent
	AMAZON-3	Worker 3	M	Pick/Stow	2020	Permanent
	AMAZON-4	Worker 4	M	Amnesty Responder. Basic troubleshooting of AGVs	2017	Permanent

(continued)

Table 2.4 (continued)

Company	Interview code	Occupational title	Sex	Main task	Company Seniority (year of beginning)	Contract
	AMAZON-5	IT specialist	M	Director of the Advanced Technology department at the European level. Development and implementation of automation technology for logistics operations	2017	Permanent
	AMAZON-6	Safety manager	M	Safety Manager for Southern Europe (IT, FRA, ES)	2017	Permanent
	AMAZON-7	HR manager	M	Senior HR Manager for the sites of Passo Corese and Colleferro	2017	Permanent
Poste Italiane	POSTE-1	Worker 1	F	Mail sorter/ AGV operator	2017	Permanent
	POSTE-2	Worker 2	M	Mail sorter/ AGV operator	2013	Permanent
	POSTE-3	Worker 3	F	Mail sorter/ AGV operator	2008	Permanent
	POSTE-4	Worker 4	F	Mail sorter/ AGV operator	2005	Permanent
	POSTE-5	IT Specialist	M	Software and Hardware integration of new technologies	2014	Permanent
	POSTE-6	HR Manager	M	Plant HR director	2006	Permanent

(continued)

Table 2.4 (continued)

Company	Interview code	Occupational title	Sex	Main task	Company Seniority (year of beginning)	Contract
	POSTE-7	Trade union official	M	Senior officer of one of the three representative confederal unions	//	//
Philip Morris	PMMTB-1	Worker/ supervisor	M	Supervisor Logistic Automation. Responsible for AGV management and maintenance	2017	Permanent
	PMMTB-2	Global operation manager	M	Responsible for the worldwide continuous improvement in logistic and warehousing operations	2016	Permanent
	PMMTB-3	HR manager	M	Responsible for HR department for PMI Italy and PMI-MTB	2010	Permanent
	PMMTB-4	Factory services manager	F	Oversees coordination with subcontractors in the plant	2014	Permanent
	PMMTB-5	IT specialist/ manager	F	Supervises software and hardware integration in the site	2009	Permanent

(continued)

Table 2.4 (continued)

Company	Interview code	Occupational title	Sex	Main task	Company Seniority (year of beginning)	Contract
	PMMTB-6	Operation manager	M	Manages the primary and secondary departments	2013	Permanent
	PMMTB-7	IT specialist/manager	M	Oversee the informatic and connectivity infrastructure in three countries: IT, D, A	2014	Permanent
	PMMTB-8	Global education and training manager	M	Responsible for a global program for the implementation of lean production	2019	Permanent

References

Alimahomed-Wilson, J., & Reese, E. (Eds.). (2020). *The cost of free shipping: Amazon in the global economy*. Pluto Press.

Allen, W. B. (1997). The logistics revolution and transportation. *Annals of the American Academy of Political and Social Science, 553*(1), 106–116. https://doi.org/10.1177/0002716297553001010

Allison, J. E., & Reese, E. (2023). *Unsustainable. Amazon, warehousing, and the politics of exploitation*. University of California Press.

Appelbaum, R., & Lichtenstein, N. (2006). A new world of retail supremacy: Supply chains and workers' chains in the age of Walmart. *International Labor and Working-Class History, 70*(Fall), 106–125. https://doi.org/10.1017/S0147547906000184

Autor, D. H. (2015). Why are there still so many jobs? The history and future of workplace automation. *Journal of Economic Perspectives, 29*(3), 3–30. https://doi.org/10.1257/jep.29.3.3

Barthel, G., & Rottenbach, J. (2017). Reelle Subsumtion und Insubordination im Zeitalter der digitalen Maschinerie: Mit-Untersuchung der Streikenden bei Amazon in Leipzig. *PROKLA. Zeitschrift Für Kritische Sozialwissenschaft, 47*(187), 249–270. https://doi.org/10.32387/prokla.v47i187.144

Benanav, A. (2020). *Automation and the future of work*. Verso.

Benvegnú, C., Haidinger, B., & Sacchetto, D. (2018). Restructuring labour relations and employment in the European logistics sector: Unions' responses to a segmented workforce. In V. Doellgast, N. Lillie, & V. Pulignano (Eds.), *Reconstructing solidarity: Labour unions, precarious work, and the politics of institutional change in Europe*. Oxford Academic. https://doi.org/10.1093/oso/9780198791843.003.0004

Bonacich, E., & Wilson, J. B. (2011). *Getting the goods. Ports, labor, and the logistics revolution*. Cornell University Press.

Boreham, P., Parker, R., Thompson, P., & Hall, R. (2008). *New technology @ Work*. Taylor and Francis.

Braverman, H. (1974). *Labor and monopoly capital: The degradation of work in the twentieth century*. Monthly Review Press.

Brunn, S. D. (Ed.). (2006). *Wal-Mart world: The world's biggest corporation in the global economy*. Routledge.

Burawoy, M. (1978). Toward a marxist theory of the labor process: Braverman and beyond. *Politics & Society, 8*(3–4), 247–312. https://doi.org/10.1177/003232927800800301

Carbonell, J. S. (2022). *Le futur du travail*. Éditions Amsterdam.

Cirillo, V., Massimo, F. S., Rinaldini, M., Staccioli, J., & Virgillito, M. E. (2023). Monopoly power upon the world of work: A workplace analysis in the logistic segment under automation. *LEM Working Paper Series*, 44. https://www.lem.sssup.it/WPLem/2023-44.html

Cirillo, V., Rinaldini, M., Staccioli, J., & Virgillito, M. E. (2021). Technology vs. workers: The case of Italy's Industry 4.0 factories. *Structural Change and Economic Dynamics, 56*, 166–183. https://doi.org/10.1016/j.strueco.2020.09.007

Cirillo, V., Rinaldini, M., Virgillito, M.E., Divella, M., Manicardi, C., Massimo, F. S., Cetrulo, A., Costantini, E., Moro, A., & Staccioli, J. (2022). *Case studies of automation in services. A workplace analysis on logistics, cleaning and health sectors in Italy*, Publications Office of the European Union, Luxembourg, 2022. https://doi.org/10.2760/347087. JRC129691.

Delfanti, A. (2021). Machinic dispossession and augmented despotism: Digital work in an Amazon warehouse. *New Media & Society, 23*(1), 39–55. https://doi.org/10.1177/1461444819891613

Edwards, P., & Ramirez, P. (2016). When should workers embrace or resist new technology? *New Technology, Work and Employment, 31*(2), 99–113. https://doi.org/10.1111/ntwe.12067

Gupta, S., Drave, V. A., Bag, S., & Luo, Z. (2019). Leveraging smart supply chain and information system agility for supply chain flexibility. *Information Systems Frontiers, 21*(3), 547–564. https://doi.org/10.1007/s10796-019-09901-5

Gutelius, B., & Theodore, N. (2019). *The future of warehouse work: Technological change in the U.S. Logistics Industry.* UC Berkeley Labor Center. http://laborcenter.berkeley.edu/future-of-warehouse-work/

Hammerling, J. H. F. (2022). *Technological change in five industries: Threats to jobs, wages, and working conditions.* UC Berkeley Labor Center. https://laborcenter.berkeley.edu/technological-change-in-five-industries/

Hocquelet, M. (2020). The impact of digital technology on skills in logistics warehouses. *Training & Employment, 145,* 4. https://shs.hal.science/halshs-02975508

Kassem, S. (2023). *Work and alienation in the platform economy. Amazon and the power of organization.* Bristol University Press.

Klumpp, M., & Zijm, H. (2019). Logistics innovation and social sustainability: How to prevent an artificial divide in human-computer interaction. *Journal of Business Logistics, 40*(3), 265–278. https://doi.org/10.1111/jbl.12198

Knights, D., & Willmott, H. (Eds.). (1990). *Labour process theory: Studies in the labour process.* Macmillan.

Koh, L. Y., & Yuen, K. F. (2022). Emerging competencies for logistics professionals in the digital era: A literature review. *Frontiers in Psychology, 13,* 965748. https://doi.org/10.3389/fpsyg.2022.965748

Lee, T. L., Tapia, M., Aranzaes, C. L., Sapre, S. R., Shimek, S., Pinto, S., & Bustamante, A. R. (2024). The militarization of employment relations: Racialized surveillance and worker control in amazon fulfillment centers. *Work and Occupations, 0*(0). https://doi.org/10.1177/07308884241292733

Lichtenstein, N. (2009). *The retail revolution: How Wal-Mart created a brave new world of business.* Metropolitan Books.

Massimo, F. S. (2020). Burocrazie Algoritmiche. Limiti e Astuzie Della Razionalizzazione Digitale in Due Stabilimenti Amazon. *Etnografia e Ricerca Qualitativa 1/2020* (pp. 53–78). https://doi.org/10.3240/96824

Massimo, F. S. (2024). *Mobilising work and demobilising labour under contemporary monopoly capitalism: A comparative study of the labour process and industrial relations in Amazon's logistics network.* PhD Thesis, Paris: Institut d'études politiques de Paris-Sciences Po/Centre de sociologie des organisations. https://theses.hal.science/tel-04778236

McKinsey. (2023). *Digital logistics: Technology race gathers momentum.* https://www.mckinsey.com/capabilities/operations/our-insights/digital-logistics-technology-race-gathersmomentum#/

Montobbio, F., Staccioli, J., Virgillito, M. E., & Vivarelli, M. (2022). Robots and the origin of their labour-saving impact. *Technological Forecasting and Social Change, 174,* 121122. https://doi.org/10.1016/j.techfore.2021.121122

Montobbio, F., Staccioli, J., Virgillito, M. E., & Vivarelli, M. (2024). Labour-saving automation: A direct measure of occupational exposure. *World Economy, 47*(1), 332–361. https://doi.org/10.1111/twec.13522

Mourtzis, D., & Doukas, M. (2012). Decentralized manufacturing systems review: Challenges and outlook. *Logistics Research, 5*, 113–121. https://doi.org/10.1007/s12159-012-0085-x

Newsome, K., Thompson, P., & Commander, J. (2013). You monitor performance at every hour: Labour and the management of performance in the supermarket supply chain. *New Technology, Work and Employment, 28*(1), 1–15. https://doi.org/10.1111/ntwe.12000

Petrovic, M., & Hamilton, G. G. (2006). Making global markets: Wal-Mart and its suppliers. In N. Lichtenstein (Ed.), *Wal-Mart: The face of twenty-first-century capitalism* (pp. 102–141). The New Press.

Sigov, A., Ratkin, L., Ivanov, L. A., & Da Xu, L. (2022). Emerging enabling technologies for industry 4.0 and beyond". *Information Systems Frontiers* [in press]. https://doi.org/10.1007/s10796-021-10213-w

Strandhagen, J. O., Vallandingham, L. R., Fragapane, G., Strandhagen, J. W., Stangeland, A. B. H., & Sharma, N. (2017). Logistics 4.0 and emerging sustainable business models. *Advances in Manufacturing, 5*(4), 359–369. https://doi.org/10.1007/s40436-017-0198-1

Thompson, P., & Laaser, K. (2021). Beyond technological determinism: Revitalising labour process analyses of technology, capital and labour. *Work in the Global Economy, 1*(1–2), 139–159. https://doi.org/10.1332/273241721X16276384832119

CHAPTER 3

Between Empowering and Risk: Organizational Change and Professional Upskilling Through Digital Health Technologies

Eleonora Costantini, Marialuisa Divella, Caterina Manicardi, and Matteo Rinaldini

Abstract This chapter describes some of the trajectories of recent technological advances in the Italian healthcare sector and their implications for work and workplace organization. Through qualitative analysis, including

---

E. Costantini (✉) · M. Rinaldini
Marco Biagi Foundation, University of Modena and Reggio Emilia, Modena, Italy
e-mail: eleonora.costantini@unimore.it

M. Divella
University of Bari 'Aldo Moro', Bari, Italy

C. Manicardi
Institute of Economics, Sant'Anna School of Advanced Studies, Pisa, Italy

M. Rinaldini
University of Modena and Reggio Emilia, Reggio Emilia, Italy

© The Author(s), under exclusive license to Springer Nature Switzerland AG 2025
V. Cirillo et al. (eds.), *Technology and Work in Services*,
https://doi.org/10.1007/978-3-031-88149-7_3

semi-structured interviews with various professionals, visits to different hospitals and clinics, and desk research, we focus on digital technologies for remote patient monitoring and virtual care. Particular attention is devoted to how these medical innovations have altered the routines and tasks of health professionals, as well as the array of organizational rearrangements occurring at the workplace level.

Keywords Healthcare · Remote patient monitoring · Virtual care · Work organization · Case studies

3.1 Introduction

In the past decade, the use of automation and digital technologies has extended into various, less standardized service industries such as healthcare and medicine. The health and social care sector—one of the largest industries in Europe, employing approximately 11% of all workers (EU OSHA, 2022a)—has witnessed the development of various technological solutions aimed at implementing digital communications and virtual consultations, remote diagnostics and patients monitoring, semi-autonomous service robots, robotic surgery, artificial intelligence, and machine learning. These technologies are currently experiencing an uptake phase in this field, albeit with considerable variability (Marques & Ferreira, 2020). The spectrum ranges from robots and artificial intelligence, to various types of digital communication devices for remote patient monitoring and the virtual provision of patient care, which are more widely adopted.

Technological advancements in the healthcare industry are increasingly addressing the socio-economic shifts of the twenty-first century, such as an aging population and the increased mobility of citizens combined with a renewed attention to fiscal budget discipline. Technological adoption in this sector aims to respond to the rising demand for long-term care by facilitating the management of chronic conditions, enabling disease prevention through continuous health monitoring, and allowing regular communication with care providers despite geographical distances—all while controlling costs (Litwin, 2020). Greater access to healthcare and the continuous collection of health data also requires adequate IoT solutions to process and store large volumes of information without overburdening doctors and health professionals (Stroumpos et al., 2023).

Although the European Strategic Plan 2019–2024 identified digital health as a strategic priority, prior to 2020, remote health monitoring solutions and telemedicine encountered numerous obstacles, from sociocultural and institutional constraints to organizational and technological barriers. However, demographic shifts and an increasing financial pressure on the European health systems—with the necessity for many hospitals to reduce costs and improve efficiency—led to gradually re-evaluating the need for remote health monitoring and telehealth consultations. Then, the outbreak of the Covid-19 pandemic fueled the adoption process (Agarwal et al., 2010; Jaumotte et al., 2023).

This chapter describes some of the trajectories of recent technological advances in the healthcare sector and their implications for work and workplace organization of healthcare personnel. Through qualitative analysis, including semi-structured interviews with various professionals, visits to different hospitals and clinics, and desk research, we focus on digital technologies for remote patient monitoring and virtual care. Particular attention is devoted to how these medical innovations have altered the routines and tasks of health professionals, as well as the array of organizational rearrangements occurring at the workplace level. Acknowledging that the development and use of technology mutually shape each other, our study can also enhance our understanding on the ongoing dynamics of medical innovation and future lines of scientific advancement (Rosenberg, 1994; Consoli & Mina, 2009).

Specifically, our research studies the implementation of technologies for both chronicity and emergency care across Italian hospitals located in different regions, allowing us to examine the presence of institutional factors that might either hinder or facilitate technology adoption. In fact, the Italian National Health Service (NHS) is funded through corporate and value-added tax revenues collected by the central government and distributed to regional governments. These regional governments are responsible for organizing and delivering health services, though they must ensure to their residents a minimum standard of care as defined by the central government (Donatini, 2020). From a research perspective, the impact of digital tools on automating various aspects or stages of healthcare provision is profound, extending beyond mere job replacement.

In healthcare, *automation* may evoke a shift from traditional, in-person medical care and assessments conducted by professionals to the use of advanced digital technologies that facilitate remote monitoring and patient diagnosis. However, this shift is largely a process of digitization rather than one of full automation. Remote monitoring devices, for instance, primarily act as digital platforms that streamline and optimize workflows without fully replacing human workers. These tools often require complementary human skills, making it difficult to draw clear boundaries between them. As distinct yet converging technologies, they blur the lines between automation, digitization, and device interconnectivity. Moreover, in the investigation, we acknowledge that the outcomes of technology integration are not entirely predefined or predictable. The actual impact depends on the specific type of technology adopted and its modalities of deployment and integration, which are shaped by the inherent characteristics of the healthcare sector (Litwin, 2022). Nevertheless, their integration has significant implications for the roles and skillsets of healthcare professionals, influencing both work organization and overall job quality.

The remainder of this chapter is structured as follows: in the next section, we provide a brief review of extant literature and motivate the relevance of our research; Sects. 3.2 and 3.3 details the research methodology, including a description of the technologies adopted and the adopting organizations; Sect. 3.3 presents and discusses the main findings, while the last section synthesizes the insights and main implications of the findings, providing a closing summary of the chapter.

3.1.1 Digital Technologies and Changes in the Italian Health Care Sector

In the evolving landscape of the labor market, the advent of digital technologies and automation has spurred extensive research into their impact. However, socio-economic studies in this field are largely centered on the impact of technology on job quantity rather than on quality, due to the absence of a reliable framework for accurately assessing several key aspects, such as the degree of new technology penetration, the specific scope of applications, and the occupations and functions most exposed (Montobbio et al., 2022).

3.1.2 Digitalization and Automation of Healthcare Technological Solutions

Although healthcare has been a key industry undergoing digital transformation since the mid-twentieth century, particularly in the United States, the adoption of these technologies is often still in its early stages, resulting in a scarcity of data for comprehensive analysis (Eden et al., 2018; Litwin, 2020). However, the disruptive impact of the Covid-19 pandemic on national health systems and remote work (OECD, 2023; Eurofound, 2020) boosted the debate on leveraging digital technologies to maintain the quality and affordability of care services, while avoiding escalating health costs and hampering health personnel's working conditions. In fact, as William L. Kissick (1994) suggests in his "Medicine's Dilemmas: Infinite Needs Versus Finite Resources," cost containment, patient access and care quality are the three core objectives that shape the healthcare sector's performance and drive technological change. These three elements form what he calls the "Iron Triangle of Health Care," where inherent trade-offs make it difficult to improve one without compromising the others. However, many scholars have emphasized the role of technology in alleviating these *iron* constraints and leading to comprehensive improvements.

A study by the European Agency for Safety and Health at Work (EU-OSHA, 2022b) carried out in 13 European Countries, combining consultation with competent national authorities, interviews with experts and a systematic literature review, shows a high number of automated or digitally supported tasks in the sector of human health and social work activities. AI frequently aids medical diagnoses, enhancing the precision of doctors' work, while robotics is commonly used for lifting objects and people, with additional support for movements like walking. Also, Wireless Body Area Networks are emerging in healthcare for real-time monitoring, which benefits chronic patients and potentially reduces hospital visits, although cost remains the main obstacle to their diffusion in both high- and low-income countries (Dhanvijay et al., 2019).

Scholars have also started devoting attention to the impact of healthcare technologies on organizational dimensions, studying the influence on those structures, processes, and hierarchies that govern how tasks and responsibilities are allocated within healthcare institutions. This dimension is closely tied to how power is distributed across different roles and departments, pointing to the authority, control, and decision-making capacity held by managers and health professionals.

A systematic literature review by Kraus et al. (2021) identifies five key clusters of research on the digital transformation of healthcare globally, which include organizational factors, managerial implications, impacts on workforce practice, and socio-economic considerations. The advent of technologies like the Internet of Things (IoT), artificial intelligence (AI), and robotics disrupts the traditional healthcare structure by reshaping how work is allocated and is shifting the balance of power among professionals. For instance, with increased reliance on digital tools, certain tasks traditionally performed by physicians or radiologists may be reallocated to nurses or automated systems. This redistribution challenges the existing hierarchies within healthcare, altering the control and influence that specific roles hold over clinical decisions and patient care. Additionally, Kraus and colleagues note that the slow pace of digital transformation in healthcare, compared to other industries, stems from barriers such as concerns about data security, the lack of expertise in health data analytics, and doubts about data reliability.

In Italy, the country where we carried out the research, the legal framework acknowledges telemedicine services as both televisit and teleassistance, based on remote interaction between the professional and the patient, teleconsultation among physicians to discuss and treat clinical cases, and telemonitoring for transmitting patient symptom scores and physiological data (Ministero della Salute, 2020). It is emphasized that these services are designed to complement, rather than substitute, the in-person delivery of medical care (Presidenza del Consiglio dei Ministri, 2021).

The Milan's Politecnico Digital Healthcare Observatory has been analyzing the digitalization of the National Health Service (SSN) for many years. Their 2022 survey data collected among health managers, GPs, specialized doctors, nurses, patients, caregivers, and citizens reveals widespread use of technologies supporting home care patients and telemedicine services. Health apps and wearable devices for monitoring clinical parameters have been used, respectively, by 38% and 29% of the interviewed patients, while 39% of specialist doctors and 41% of GPs state they have used telemedicine services, and 30% and 39% have resorted to telemonitoring (Agenda Digitale, 2022). According to de Belvis and coauthors, IT supports over 60% of health facility activities, mostly for diagnostic imaging—particularly for radiology tests and surgical operating rooms—while online booking and payment systems are underutilized by the population despite being available in over 75% of NHS facilities (de Belvis et al., 2022).

3.1.3 Institutional Challenges in Healthcare Digitization

The research is carried out within the institutional framework of the Italian National Health Service (SSN), a decentralized system where each Region independently plans and manages healthcare services to ensure that essential levels of care, as defined by the State, are delivered within their territories. This decentralized structure has created disparities across regions in terms of healthcare resource allocation, digital infrastructure, and the adoption of new technologies, exacerbating unequal access to services for patients based on their region of residence (Ferrera, 1995; Pizzuti et al., 2022). The SSN operates under increasing pressure due to financial constraints that overburden health professionals, lead to workforce shortages, and pave the way to increased private sector involvement, with these factors likely playing a role in shaping the adoption and integration of digital solutions across the healthcare system.

Over the past twenty-five years, the total health expenditure has grown by an average of +2.6% annually, lagging behind the +3.8% growth seen in EU-ante 1995. In the period 2010–2019, the public share of total expenditure on health declined from 78.5 to 73.9% (WHO, 2022). While the National Recovery and Resilience Plan aims to expand SSN capacity through significant investment in new facilities, how these facilities will be staffed remains uncertain due to the shortages of health professionals and budget constraints (Ufficio Parlamentare Bilancio, 2019).

To address these challenges, the 19th Health Report by the Center for Economic Research Applied to Healthcare (CREA Sanità, 2022) advocates for urgent refinancing of the system and reengineering of services through digital technologies. This transformation should be aimed at respecting citizens' «time preservation» by shortening waiting lists and avoiding bureaucratic complexities. The report also remarks that the principle of universality should be extended from the scope of «prevention-rehabilitation» to the inclusion of «dependency/chronicity» and «end of life/long-term care». However, despite recent national and European legislative efforts to promote digital transformation, progress has remained sluggish due to interoperability issues, regional disparities in reimbursement schemes, and limited resources for implementation

(Agenda Digitale, 2022). These factors contribute to the uneven pace of digital transformation and highlight the need for more focused efforts on overcoming institutional obstacles.

3.1.4 Recent Trends in the Italian Healthcare Labor Market: Wage Compression and Labor Shortages

The institutional context has straightforward implications on healthcare work, with recent trends highlighting a growing strain on the workforce and stagnation of wages. In Italy alone, healthcare employment encompasses 1.4 million individuals, representing 5.7% of total employment, with more than 660,000 in the National Health Service (CERGAS, 2017). In Germany and the United Kingdom, the current salary of physicians adjusted for purchasing power parity is respectively 79% and 40% higher than that in Italy. Similarly, nurses in Germany, Switzerland, and the United Kingdom earn annual salaries 56%, 46.2%, and 20.0% higher than those in Italy (OECD, 2022).

Compared to European averages, the number of doctors in the country is relatively high, while there is a scarcity of nurses (Istat, 2020). However, the number of public hospital physicians, nurses, and GPs is now decreasing most likely due to the declining investment in health personnel and related hiring freezes since 2010, coupled with an intensification of their workload and overall deteriorating working conditions (de Belvis et al., 2022; Pavolini, 2020).According to the 2023 C.R.E.A. Report, many young professionals opt to work abroad or on a per diem basis (*lavoro a gettone*) rather than being organic to the SSN in order to avoid long hours and excessive workloads (CREA Sanità, 2022).

The 19th Health Report by the Center for Economic Research Applied to Healthcare in 2023 emphasizes the waning confidence in the Italian NHS among both citizens/patients and healthcare professionals over the past decade. Notably, out-of-pocket and intermediated (i.e., through health funds and insurance) spending has steadily increased, alongside a growing preference for hospitalizations and surgery in accredited private facilities (from 24.8% to 27.1% and from 33.4% to 33.8% respectively in the period 2017–2022).

Against this background, our research focuses on the adoption and integration of technologies for remote monitoring and virtual patient care in hospitals across different regions. It lies at the core of the ongoing debate on digitization and automation of clinical services and work processes in healthcare, as these technologies have the potential to transform both the patient experience and clinical practice. Our fieldwork is also able to capture the workplace-specific, non-economic drivers of behavior and decision-making. In fact, differently from manufacturing, the healthcare sector's idiosyncratic features in terms of organizational practices, tasks and skills require a nuanced approach to implementing ICT and robots. Beyond simple aggregate data analysis, the complex nature of healthcare work—including unique work tasks, skill sets, and organizational practices—calls for in-depth qualitative research into the specific ways in which these technologies are implemented across different entities. Such an approach should yield richer insights and deeper understanding of the diverse perspectives on this technological adoption and integration (Yin, 2014; Sostero, 2020).

Interestingly, the healthcare professionals undergoing the most significant upskilling due to the implementation of the technologies under study are also those enduring the highest levels of workplace overload and receiving the lowest pay—namely, emergency doctors, nurses, and IT specialists. This result, which will be further elaborated in the following paragraphs, hints at the potential of technology adoption to empower professionals at the lower to middle levels of the hierarchy, enhancing their professional recognition and, hopefully, improving their compensation (Autor et al., 2003).

3.2 The Technologies of Interest, Selected Case Studies, and Methodology

3.2.1 Technologies of Interest

In this chapter, we focus on remote patient monitoring technologies, as these are among the most widely adopted innovations within the healthcare sector. The decision to prioritize these technologies stems from their more prevalent integration into healthcare systems compared to other more niche innovations, such as robotics and certain applications of artificial intelligence. While these latter technologies are often still in trial phases and less frequently adopted, remote monitoring tools have seen broader, real-world implementation. By selecting technologies that are more widely used, we aim to provide a more representative perspective on their transformative impact and the broader implications for healthcare professionals. Hence, for our qualitative analysis, we choose three distinct technologies and examine their application in two different contexts, allowing us to assess their influence on work practices and organizational dynamics in diverse settings.

The first technology is represented by remote monitoring systems for implantable heart devices. These systems enable healthcare providers to assess the status of a patient's cardiac implants, such as pacemakers and implantable cardioverter-defibrillators, without requiring in-person visits. Typically, these technologies involve a home monitoring unit or the patient's own smart device, which communicates with the implanted device to collect data on its functionality as well as the patient's cardiac activity. This information—such as battery status, heart rhythm, and a history of any events like arrhythmias or delivered device therapies—is transmitted to the healthcare provider via a secure network. As a result, remote monitoring facilitates the optimization of device settings, timely detection of potential issues, and early intervention if a patient's condition changes. This approach not only reduces hospitalizations but also enhances patient care and assistance, particularly for those who live far from their specialists or face mobility challenges.

The second technology is the telestroke system, a telemedicine device that enables remote diagnosis and treatment of stroke patients. It connects patients in rural or underserved areas with neurologists or stroke specialists through videoconferencing and data-sharing technologies. When a patient presents stroke symptoms at a hospital, clinicians can use the telestroke system to quickly consult with specialists, even if they are miles away, sharing critical data and images (such as CT scans) in real-time. This significantly reduces the time to treatment, which is crucial for improving stroke outcomes. As a result, only the most severe cases requiring intensive treatment are centralized in the stroke unit of the main hospital, while all other patients can receive treatment and hospitalization at peripheral facilities.

The third technology consists of remote monitoring devices for cardiovascular conditions and defibrillation, used onboard advanced emergency vehicles. These are critical tools for pre-hospital care, enabling timely and effective medical intervention before patients reach the hospital. These devices typically include automated external defibrillators that can automatically diagnose life-threatening cardiac arrhythmias and administer an electric shock to restore normal heart rhythm; ECG (electrocardiogram) monitors, essential for identifying arrhythmias, myocardial infarctions, and other cardiac conditions during transit; vital signs monitors, which track key parameters like blood pressure and oxygen saturation; and telemedicine systems that transmit real-time data, including ECG's, to hospitals or remote cardiologists for immediate review and guidance on treatment. The integration of these devices into emergency vehicles transforms them into mobile units capable of delivering sophisticated medical care, enabling first responders to initiate life-saving treatments promptly and to make informed decisions about the immediate care needs of patients, while they are transferred to the hospital.

As we will explore in greater detail later in this chapter, these three technologies can be categorized into two main groups: one focused on chronic disease management and the other on emergency intervention. This classification highlights the distinct roles that these technologies play in supporting healthcare delivery, with the first group (remote monitoring systems for implantable heart devices) aimed at providing ongoing monitoring and care for patients with chronic conditions, therefore allowing healthcare providers to make timely adjustments to treatment plans; while the second group (telestroke and remote monitoring devices onboard advance emergency vehicles) emphasizes rapid response and treatment during emergencies, facilitating diagnosis and intervention to improve patient outcomes in critical situations.

3.2.2 Selected Case Studies

The three technologies under examination have been observed in three concrete cases of adoption across two Italian regions.

The first two were studied at the Santa Maria Nuova Hospital in Reggio Emilia, located in the Emilia Romagna region. This prominent local healthcare provider is at the forefront of technological adoption within Italy's National Health System and has made advance in telemedicine integration, particularly in remote monitoring for implantable heart devices and telestroke, which served as the basis for the first case study.

Focusing on the remote monitoring of implantable heart devices, the Santa Maria Nuova Hospital has been utilizing this technology since 2014, with its advantages particularly highlighted during the pandemic. The restrictions on movement and clinic visits necessitated by the pandemic led the hospital's electrophysiology unit to establish a "virtual clinic," which now oversees the care of over 1,200 cardiac patients. This remote system enables immediate access to data from implanted heart devices, significantly reducing the need for hospital and emergency visits. Additionally, it streamlines the generation of annual reports by seamlessly integrating them into patients' electronic health records. While this remote monitoring framework has effectively decreased in-person consultations and hospital admissions, its implementation required substantial organizational commitment. A critical aspect of this effort was the establishment of an in-house technical support team and the development of a digital communication infrastructure integrated with the regional healthcare system, which has ensured a more robust and effective remote patient monitoring program.

The telestroke system, introduced in 2019, enables remote diagnosis and treatment of stroke patients, enhancing collaboration with emergency services in peripheral areas and centralizing neurological care at the Santa Maria Nuova Hospital. This centralization involves the areas of Castelnuovo Monti and Guastalla. While the system was designed to connect the northern and southern parts of the province, operational constraints in the northern area have limited its full implementation. At the time of the interviews, the telestroke system operated exclusively at Guastalla Hospital, which does not have its own neurology unit. This arrangement allows neurologists from Santa Maria Nuova Hospital to conduct remote evaluations, although these consultations are not available during night-time due to limited staff and neurologist availability. Prior to the implementation of telestroke, emergency doctors at outlying hospitals relied on phone calls to consult neurologists—a method that often led to misdiagnoses due to the complexity of stroke symptoms. The integration of telestroke did not require significant infrastructure investments; it merely involved setting up appropriate spaces equipped with high-quality monitors and cameras. However, organizational challenges, such as the need for rescheduling and staffing shortages, have hindered broader adoption. For example, Castelnuovo Monti Hospital, which was positioned to become another telestroke site even before the pandemic, has faced staffing issues that have stalled its pilot phase since.

The third case study focuses on ASUR Marche, a regional health authority that encompasses five territorial units known as "vast areas" within the Marche region. Our analysis examines "vast area 2," which includes the Riuniti Torrette Hospital in Ancona and the peripheral health districts of Fabriano, Jesi, and Senigallia. In 2015, the region expanded the deployment of the Lifepak 15 technology system across this area.

This advanced system, equipped with ECG and defibrillation capabilities, connects emergency vehicles to a central station at Riuniti Torrette Hospital, enabling prompt and automated diagnoses of heart attacks. The Lifepak 15 setup allows ambulance staff to perform ECGs on-site and collaborate with cardiologists at the central station for real-time evaluations. This collaboration increases diagnostic accuracy and accelerates the initiation of life-saving care. Between the beginning of 2021 and September of the same year, the system transmitted 1,350 ECGs, resulting in 91 direct surgical admissions, which exemplifies its efficiency in triaging patients for expedited care while conserving hospital resources. Despite the operational success of this technology, it did not require significant investments in network infrastructure or hardware, aside from establishing a data acquisition hub within the cardiology unit. However, personnel shortages present similar challenges as those observed with telestroke technology; the availability of cardiologists remains a critical factor in fully harnessing the capabilities of the Lifepak 15 system.

3.2.3 Methodology

We employ a qualitative analysis to explore the transformative effects of specific technologies on the healthcare employment landscape within selected public hospitals in the Emilia Romagna and Marche regions of Italy. Utilizing semi-structured interviews with various professionals, complemented by field visits to the adopting organizations and comprehensive desk research, we examine the impacts of these technologies. Our investigation focuses around four key areas: the effect of technology on service provision; its influence on organizational structures and workflows; potential changes in job quality; and the redefinition of professional tasks. By integrating these dimensions, our study aims to dissect the ongoing evolution in healthcare service delivery, highlighting how these new tools are increasingly integrated into day-to-day operations.

All interviews have been meticulously recorded and transcribed, with a detailed assessment of the interviewees' profiles provided in the Appendix. We employ a multi-hierarchical coding system to distil the conversations from theoretical and abstract constructs into tangible insights. This method, grounded in the work of Alvesson and Karreman (2011), facilitates a dynamic interchange between theory and practical findings. It enables a thorough analysis that enriches our study by deepening insights through a comparative evaluation across different health organizations.

More in detail, our initial semi-structured interview at Santa Maria Nuova Hospital has involved the head of the "Complex Structure ICT and Telematics Service" of the Reggio Emilia Health Agency (ASL), providing a comprehensive perspective on the processes of technology adoption and implementation. He has played a crucial role in arranging subsequent interviews, including a video conference with the chief of the neurology unit. In our examination of remote monitoring, we have consulted both the director of the cardiology unit and a cardiology technician with direct experience using the technology. To conclude our interviews, we revisited the head of the Complex Structure ICT and Telematics Service to gather insights on the selected technologies for our case study, as well as the clinical engineer responsible for their implementation.

For the telestroke technology, we have engaged in discussions with the head of the neurology department (via video interview), who was instrumental in promoting and coordinating the adoption process, as well as with a digital device maintainer. To gain further insights into the organizational changes related to the introduction of telestroke, we have expanded our inquiries to peripheral hospitals, including Guastalla, where telestroke was in operation, and Castelnuovo Monti, where it was not. Utilizing a snowball sampling technique, we have interviewed the telestroke physician in Guastalla and a physician in Castelnuovo Monti.

Our inquiry at Riuniti Torrette Hospital has involved in-person discussions and an examination of the emergency department's operations. The primary interview has been conducted with the medical director of the emergency department, who also serves as IT specialist responsible for the technology implementation. This interview provides a detailed overview of the technology's functionality and its integration into emergency processes. We were able to observe the Lifepak 15 technology in action on board the advanced emergency vehicles. Subsequently, we conducted semi-structured interviews with the human resources manager, two emergency physicians, ambulance nurses, and the medical director of the cardiac intensive care unit. These discussions were aimed at capturing a wide range of perspectives and roles in the integration and implementation of the technologies under examination.

To enhance the presentation of the results, we chose to describe the changes brought about by the introduction of the telestroke technology and Lifepak 15 technology system together, while the remote monitoring of implantable devices was discussed separately (Table 3.1).

Table 3.1 Summary of technologies and contexts of implementation

Contexts of implementation	Technologies	
	Chronicity management	Emergency treatment
Santa Maria Nuova	Remote monitoring of implantable heart devices	Telestroke
ASUR Marche		Lifepack 15—defibrillation employed onboard advanced emergency vehicles and remote monitoring devices for cardiovascular conditions

As previously mentioned, the three technologies in question can be categorized into two main groups (Table 3.1): one focusing on chronic disease management and the other on emergency intervention. This classification, which emerged during the field research phase, is valuable as it helps to synthesize and clarify the results. It underscores the distinct roles these technologies play in enhancing healthcare delivery, namely "Chronicity management" (providing continuous monitoring and care for patients with chronic conditions) or "Emergency treatment" (rapid response and intervention during emergencies).

3.3 Findings: Digitalization and Changes in Organizational Processes and Working Conditions of Healthcare Personnel

As mentioned above, although the introduction of these technologies did not require notable investments in terms of network, hardware or software, some significant changes in work organization were still necessary. In particular, across all the technologies analyzed, key adjustments were identified in terms of methods (e.g., at least a partial increase in repetition and standardization for nurses, alongside potentially greater autonomy for both nurses and doctors), tools (i.e., increased use of digital technologies and need to follow specific protocols and procedures to ensure correct functioning) and task content.

3.3.1 The Remote Monitoring of Implantable Devices for Patients with Chronicity

With regard to the remote monitoring of implantable devices, the initial decision on which patients to transfer to the virtual clinic was not based on medical assessment but was only possible for those patients whose implantable heart devices allowed for remote monitoring. However, annual check-ups of implanted devices are now conducted remotely for a significant portion of cardiopathic patients undergoing treatment at the electrophysiology unit at Santa Maria Nuova. This became possible through significant organizational investment, including the hiring of a dedicated technical expert and the establishment of a new technical office for the electrophysiology division. Additionally, the administrative unit appears to play a crucial role in the operation of the televisit system, with several new tasks assigned to customer service operators. The implementation of remote monitoring for implantable devices has not only streamlined patient care but also necessitated the creation of new professional profiles. The hiring of dedicated technical experts and the establishment of a technical office for the electrophysiology unit have been key to the system's success. Moreover, the increasing responsibilities within the administrative unit highlights how technological advancements are reshaping the personnel, leading to the creation of specialized roles essential for managing innovative healthcare services.

The remote monitoring of cardiac devices is crucially dependent on daily interaction between the cardiologist and the dedicated IT division, with a positive influence in terms of additional opportunities for interaction and collaboration between colleagues at different levels of the work organization.

> The management of the devices is far easier now. I must say that technicians do a great job. Other than the routine tasks related to the technical maintenance of the devices, the relationship with providers and the daily monitoring of relevant alerts, I asked them to report to me on the number of disconnected patients every 15 days. [...] We collaborate on a daily basis; we are continuously in touch.

AUSL RE 5 – SMN, Cardiologist

Relevant changes mainly concern the task content of the technical specialists and administrative units, involving an increase in physical, intellectual, and social tasks. Indeed, significant upskilling, particularly in digital competencies, is evident. However, technical specialists have also taken on work activities previously under the responsibility of the cardiology unit, such as checking the mailbox every morning and frequently throughout the day, assessing the priority of alerts indicating potential device malfunctions or acute cardiac events in patients. In cases of low priority, intervention by the cardiologist is unnecessary: the technical specialists contact the patient and schedule an in-person appointment to restore the device's functionality. For cases of medium to high priority, they refer the matter to the cardiologist to determine the urgency of scheduling a meeting with the patient.

Also in this case, although some visits requiring more detailed clinical examinations are conducted by the cardiologist, technical specialists might also conduct the visit. Moreover, communication between the hospital and the patient is managed by the technical specialists and the administrative unit, and this communication is crucial as the patient does not receive any direct warning from the device in the event of anomalies.

> Our main activities are based on the control of the remote monitoring system; it is one of our priorities. So, every morning from Monday to Friday, one of the first things we do is to check the mailbox to see whether any alert arrived from the remote monitoring systems that patients have at home [...] one of our tasks is the technical evaluation of the type of information we receive: if the alert is a priority and deserves immediate attention, we inform the doctor [...] and the clinical decision is up to them. [...] If the alert needs further investigation, we call the patient and arrange a visit in person: the patient is then received in our clinic by us technicians and we do a preliminary check of the device [...] if it is the case, the cardiologist intervenes and finalises the visit, but it is also possible that our technical check-up is sufficient to solve the problem. ... We actually do a frequent check of the emails even while I do other activities. [...] At least half, three quarters of our time is dedicated to the technology and related tasks. From a professional point of view, it was certainly a great advantage, we as technicians also gained a lot because these remote monitoring systems are demanding and require constant updates so we keep ourselves updated along with our devices, leading to remarkable professional enrichment [...] the total workload has increased since the total number of patients has increased [...] you used to see many patients once a year, now you follow them every day so potentially there is much more work to do.

AUSL RE 4—SMN, IT specialist of cardiovascular physiopathology

The entire workload—except for carrying out the visit in the case of the most severe or controversial alerts—is maintained by tech specialists with a remarkable professional enrichment due to continuous updates concerning the functioning and applicability of the remote monitoring technology. On the contrary, cardiologists were not really impacted by the implementation of the technology.

In addition, it is conceivable that new tasks are required also for caregivers or family members, who reasonably ensure that the monitor is working or take care of the setup at home for the televisit. However, the real impact on caregivers' work is not clear since the interviews did not involve users of such technologies.

3.3.2 The Telestroke Technology System and Lifepak 15 for Emergency Treatment

Regarding the telestroke technology system and Lifepak 15, the main objective is the integration between the specialized units (neurology and hemodynamic) present in the hospitals and the peripheral units, namely the emergency room (telestroke) and the ambulance (Lifepak 15). The aim of this integration is threefold: to reduce emergency intervention time, to select the most appropriate intervention, and to minimize unnecessary transfers to the central hospital.

Through remote consultation, the involvement of the stroke expert enables the emergency medical staff at the peripheral hospital of Guastalla to accurately diagnose ischemic strokes versus hemorrhagic strokes and recommend the appropriate treatment. Ischaemic strokes typically require thrombolysis (also known as fibrinolysis), a procedure that can only be performed at Santa Maria Nuova Hospital and requires immediate transfer. Regarding Lifepak 15, based on the severity level of the call received by the emergency department, the doctors and nurses decide whether to bring the Lifepak to the emergency vehicle or not. Once on-site, they input the patient's information, apply the electrodes, and generate the ECG. If the results are clear and the machine's diagnosis aligns with their assessment, no further action is needed. However, if the condition is unclear, they consult a remote cardiologist for additional insight into the severity of the issue and to coordinate potential surgical intervention. The machine's diagnosis supports, but does not replace, the final decision of the doctor or nurse.

Although the two case studies involve diverse professional profiles and different technologies for different emergency interventions, it is possible to identify common trends in terms of working conditions. Indeed, both processes described have resulted in significant reskilling and the creation of a more collaborative working environment in which nursing and medical staff work together.

> Now the neurologist has to trust their colleagues. Initially we were afraid. [...] The practical advantage is also professional because to prepare this programme we did a very intense job training. [...] Now the staff of the peripheral hub have not only entered into the logic of evaluating a patient with the right times and methods but also that of sharing the final decision with neurologists. So there is involvement in the diagnostic and therapeutic process for a stroke that was not there before. [...] This is positive because it spreads knowledge and now the medical and nursing staff of the spoke hospital also has an exact idea of what it means to do thrombolysis, that is, to do a time-dependent therapy for a patient with a stroke.

AUSL RE 7—SMN, Neurologist

> When you are outside on the auto-infermieristica (Editor's note: an emergency vehicle staffed exclusively by nurses and equipped with medical supplies and diagnostic tools), being in contact with the cardiologist is of great help. [...] The collaboration between cardiologists and nurses is facilitated by this transmission system and is also much more reassuring in the sense that the operator who is on the territory sometimes feels a little abandoned. [...] In addition, maybe you are in a nursing emergency vehicle with no doctor on board and this becomes even more fundamental because you have telephone contact with a specialist doctor, after the transmission, who tells you exactly what to do.

ASUR MARCHE 5, Nurse

Moreover, in terms of upskilling, the implementation of telestroke technology and the associated improvement in accurate diagnosis have prompted the management of Guastalla—the peripheral hospital—to internally deploy such a procedure, leading to significant upskilling of the nursing staff, who are now required to perform more complex tasks. The usage protocol established by the Italian Hospital Directorate, in collaboration with the neurology division, permits the nursing staff to utilize the technology and conduct the visit only under the supervision of the emergency doctor. However, the option of giving nurses greater autonomy in initiating and managing telestroke as a response to the shortage of emergency doctors remains controversial. Similarly, the adoption of Lifepak 15 has resulted in significant upskilling of the nursing staff. Nurses at peripheral sites can now perform thrombolytic procedures, transmit an ECG through Lifepak 15, and liaise with cardiologists.

> Even if some colleagues do not accept it, the role of nurses will increase in importance in the coming years. [...] There still are relevant differences between regions about what nurses can or cannot do, but I think that the opposition of medical associations will not last long given the reduction in the number of emergency doctors we experience every day [...] now nurses can only transmit, they cannot do the therapy [...] there are some realities in Italy where the nurse in front of, let's say, in front of certain patients who have certain symptoms interfaces with the doctor on the basis of what is said by the nurse, the central doctor authorises them to give certain drugs, to carry out or do therapies in the within the field. Here it is not possible.

ASUR MARCHE 7, Manager of emergency divisions

> Our interaction with cardiologists is now at a high level and I must say that it represents an important learning opportunity since they support you throughout the visit and explain why they choose to do a specific action or treatment [...] However, the proper understanding of the ECG trace requires upskilling for our category. In fact, I paid for a private course on that on my own, even though I would say that experience plays a decisive role and after several months your on-the-job training would be sufficient.

ASUR MARCHE 2, Emergency Doctor

Furthermore, the adoption of both technologies appears to contribute to notable upskilling, particularly in digital competencies, as well as expanded knowledge and «learning through interaction» with colleagues, medical equipment, technology providers, and technical specialists.

In terms of the working environment, Lifepak 15 appears to have a positive impact by creating additional opportunities for interaction and collaboration among colleagues at various levels of the organizational hierarchy. Remote consultation with the cardiologist serves as psychological support for all staff aboard the emergency vehicle, whether it is a doctor-staffed «auto-medica» or a nurse-staffed «auto-infermieristica». Similarly, the use of telestroke requires an element of trust between the neurologist, who cannot be physically present during the consultation, and the on-site emergency doctor, as the legal responsibility remains with the neurologist.

> The big difference is learning how to work as a team [...] in the dynamics of traditional first aid, the neurologist arrives and the emergency doctor goes to do something else. Instead, now it is a team evaluation because one is the right arm of the other.

AUSL RE 2—SMN, IT specialist of neuropsychopathology

> We as emergency doctors had to improve our medical vocabulary in order to interact with neurologists. For example, for me there is just one type of aphasia, while for neurologists there are thousands of different shades of incapacity to speak of and in order to answer their questions, we needed to refine our language and how we perform the visit.

AUSL RE 6—GUA, Emergency Doctor

Looking at both technologies, emergency doctors and nurses are both significantly affected in terms of task content. Overall, besides a partial reduction in physical, intellectual, and social tasks performed by doctors, particularly those in emergency departments, significant changes in task content for nursing staff have been observed, with an increase in physical, intellectual, and social tasks. Additionally, both technologies lead nurses to undertake more tasks of various types without the presence of doctors. Specifically, nurses are more frequently involved in processing and monitoring information, as well as problem-solving. Moreover, they are more frequently engaged in increased interaction with doctors and in teaching and training activities. In other words, the introduction of new technologies and the resulting changes in organizational processes have led to a quantitative and qualitative increase in the tasks performed by nurses, often not formally recognized, but crucial for the functioning of the implemented intervention system.

Conversely, the emergency doctors save time related to useless transfers and dedicate more time to the diagnostic phase of the stroke patient, while the neurologists seem to have experienced a densification of tasks, although the number of centralized patients in the hub is now reduced. Moreover, the accuracy of the diagnosis is crucially dependent on the harmonization of medical language between the non-specialist and the specialist doctor to ensure effective communication of the patient's symptoms. This led to gradual on-the-job upskilling of emergency doctors.

Similarly, other operators involved, such as the technical specialists in the neurophysiopathologist unit, carry out a daily check of the machine, although this has not required further training nor the acquisition of precise digital skills.

In both cases, technology adoption does not seem to entail relevant changes in the overall level of occupation. The Lifepak 15 monitor/defibrillator, for instance, seems not to demand new hirings, as it (at least partially) responds to the lack of emergency doctors by providing nurses in emergency vehicles with a reliable technology for accurate diagnosis. On the other hand, only a few potential negative effects on the health and safety of workers have been identified, such as the weight of the Lifepak and the associated fatigue experienced by paramedics, ambulance drivers and nurses on the way to the patient's home.

The most controversial issue that has arisen is the expansion of nurses' skills, particularly in the area of medical knowledge: some medical staff are uncomfortable with nurses using the Lifepak without the presence of a doctor. Conversely, others view this as an inevitable solution to the shortage of doctors in emergency departments, a challenge many regions have already addressed by increasing the number of tasks performed by nurses. In general, this shift in duties and the change in the content of nurses' tasks have not been followed by corresponding upgrades in the contract level or remuneration. Given the large majority of female nurses, these changes in tasks and increased responsibilities for nurses, without appropriate recognition, risk increasing gender inequalities within the occupational structure of the health sector, and hindering the potential benefits of digitization for female-dominated professions.

3.3.3 Time Management as a Key Variable to Understand Techno-Organizational Changes and Their Impact on Working Conditions

In general, the introduction of new technologies has led to changes in organizational processes related to visits, diagnosis, and treatment in all the studied cases. However, these changes follow different trajectories depending on whether the technologies are used for emergency intervention in acute conditions (telestroke and Lifepak 15) or for the treatment of chronic conditions (cardiac devices and remote monitoring).

Time management appears to be the key variable in the organizational design associated with introducing new technologies: for acute conditions, speed is crucial in deciding on the most appropriate care, and the technologies adopted allow for more rapid shared decision-making in response to time-varying conditions; in the case of chronic conditions, the temporal extension and intensification of monitoring are essential dimensions guiding the planning of monitoring activities to prevent emergencies, with the adopted technologies allowing for regular and more frequent transmission of information. Based on this diversity of technology use regarding time management, different impacts on the working conditions of healthcare personnel can be identified.

In emergency-oriented work processes that involve technologies such as telestroke or Lifepak 15, peripheral site personnel (including ambulance staff) are required to maintain the equipment on an ongoing basis (requiring a skill set for maintenance activities) and to bear a greater physical workload due to handling the new technologies. On the other hand, decentralized site personnel are required to work collaboratively and build trust with professionals of different specialties. This does not mean an intensification of work, but rather an increase in its complexity. This aspect represents a great opportunity for skill development and hybridization, although there are problematic elements such as the establishment of a common language to facilitate effective information exchange—since the same medical term may have different meanings for an emergency room doctor and a neurologist—or the lack of recognition by contract or through upgrading.

At the same time, there is a contradiction between, on the one hand, the increased discretion allowed by the new techno-organizational arrangement and the consequent assumption of greater responsibility (Susskind & Susskind, 2015), and, on the other hand, the risks that different professional roles face if they do not adhere to the formal regulations and operational boundaries established by legislation. For instance, nurses may have more decision-making power when interacting with patients due to data-driven tools that support more informed decisions. This empowerment comes with an increased sense of responsibility: while nurses might have more data at their fingertips, they are also held accountable for interpreting and acting on that data. At the same time, professionals still operate within strict legal and operational frameworks. These regulations serve to protect both the patient (in the healthcare example) and the professional, but they can also limit the flexibility that new technologies promise. Not adhering to formal guidelines—regardless of the new discretion afforded by technological tools—can expose professionals to legal, financial, or reputational risks. A nurse who goes beyond standard procedure, even when empowered by technology, could face severe consequences if things go wrong. Hence, this contradiction and the need to protect themselves from legal scrutiny and professional blame may lead healthcare personnel to advocate for the standardization of procedures, thereby stiffening the spaces of flexibility that new technologies allow. This results in a kind of "self-imposed" limitation, where workers resist the full flexibility of new technologies because they are more focused on safeguarding themselves from potential fallout. The outcome is thus a paradox where the potential benefits of digitization—like efficiency, autonomy, or improved decision-making—are not fully realized because professionals resist using these tools in ways that diverge from established norms.

All this directly hints at the management challenges in effectively leveraging the potential benefits of digitization. A kind of impasse is generated between some "empowered" professional profiles and legislators who may be either committed or reluctant to ease the establishment of a new set of workplace relationships that can both secure workers and release the full potential of emerging technologies (Zuboff, 1988). This creates a challenge for managers in how to "unlock" the benefits of technological innovation while not exposing workers to undue risks. It is a delicate balance between empowering staff and enforcing compliance. Management has to navigate these complexities, while legislators must also evolve policies that reflect the realities of digital work without stifling its potential.

In work processes focused on chronic disease monitoring, instead, the introduction of new technologies has necessitated the creation of new professional roles, namely data flow management technicians, who are tasked with interacting with patients when there are no major issues or anomalies. The role of these professionals is crucial as they perform a communication function between the hospital and the patient in standard situations and act as a warning to cardiologists when a problem arises. In addition, routine device maintenance tasks are delegated to patients or, if they are not self-sufficient, to their caregivers (family members, home help, etc.). This organizational reconfiguration results in a much more standardized and routinized work process than in the past, which reduces the workload of cardiologists, but also significantly changes the work of healthcare personnel, the content of work activities and the skills required to perform them.

3.4 Conclusion

The remote monitoring of implantable devices, the telestroke, and the Lifepak15 technology are used for remote patient monitoring, real-time data, and information transfer, and for connecting the various healthcare professionals involved in decision-making processes related to diagnosis and treatment activities. These technologies have been introduced with the dual aim of improving the effectiveness of medical care and reducing associated costs. The introduction of cardiac devices and remote monitoring helps reduce the risks associated with the exacerbation of chronic conditions and the occurrence of crises, as well as reducing (but not eliminating) the time spent by healthcare personnel on routine visits. The introduction of telestroke and Lifepak15 enables rapid diagnosis and effective intervention based on specialized medical expertise, thereby reducing the risks associated with errors or delays in emergency treatment, as well as minimizing the costs associated with unnecessary transfers to central facilities or unnecessary medical procedures. None of these technologies represents a transition to full automation, but rather a digitization of healthcare services, where the human factor remains fundamental.

The research revealed some common changes across the case studies. First, the technologies adopted were not used to replace jobs or tasks previously performed by nurses or doctors. On the contrary, as clearly demonstrated by the case studies, it is often the lack of human resources that limits the further use of some of these technologies.

Second, the technologies introduced into work processes create conditions for greater collaboration between organizational units and different professional roles. Indeed, the effective use of these technologies requires a change in the management of information flows and the coordination of activities in order to improve relationships between different departments/units and between doctors, nurses, and health technicians.

Thirdly, nurses and health technicians have taken on more complex responsibilities, ranging from technical evaluations and monitoring alerts to direct patient treatment. This shift has expanded their autonomy and involvement in critical decisions, although these new tasks often conflict with formal regulations defining their professional boundaries.

Upskilling, particularly in digital and communication competencies, has been a notable consequence, with staff increasingly required to manage and interpret digital health data, interact with advanced devices, and work more closely with specialists across departments. This expanded skill set has not been accompanied by appropriate recognition or compensation also due to legislative constraints, particularly for nurses whose workload has increased without formal adjustments to their professional contracts.

Another key finding across the case studies is the centrality of time management in how these technologies have restructured work processes. In acute care settings, such as those involving telestroke and Lifepak15, speed is critical. The real-time coordination between emergency personnel and specialists facilitates rapid decision-making, enhancing both diagnostic accuracy and treatment outcomes. By contrast, in chronic care, remote monitoring technologies have extended and intensified the monitoring process, allowing for continuous oversight and early intervention. This has led to more frequent yet routine tasks for technical staff, reducing cardiologist's workload but increasing the daily responsibilities of other healthcare personnel.

Overall, since healthcare operates within the public sector in the examined context, any considerations are necessarily anchored to the prevailing national legislation. In light of the findings detailed in this study, and given the broader context outlined in the referenced book, it would be interesting to investigate whether the dimensions identified for the Italian national case are also present in other national contexts. This exploration is particularly vital given the significant impact of the national sectoral regulation on the adoption decisions of new digital technologies and on the outcomes of integrating these technologies in various settings.

Appendix

Hospital	Interview code	Professional category	Sex	Main task	Company seniority (year of beginning)	Contract
AUSL RE—Scandiano and Castelnuovo Monti Hospitals	AUSL RE 1—SCA	Emergency doctor	M	Manages the emergency service of the hospitals of Scandiano (RE) and Castelnuovo Monti (RE) and coordinate the services provided by the voluntary associations	2014	Permanent
AUSL RE—Santa Maria Nuova Hospital	AUSL RE 2—SMN	IT specialist of neurophysiopathology	M	Executes of electroencephalograms, electrocardiographs and other tracing of the activity of the nervous system under medical prescription in Santa Maria Nuova hospital (RE)	1994	Permanent
AUSL RE—Santa Maria Nuova Hospital	AUSL RE 3—SMN	IT specialist	M	Manages the digitalized processes and related data within Santa Maria Nuova hospital (RE)	2006	Permanent
AUSL RE—Santa Maria Nuova Hospital	AUSL RE 4—SMN	IT specialist of cardiovascular physiopathology	F	Manages the system of remote monitoring of implantable heart devices in Santa Maria Nuova hospital (RE)	2006	Permanent
AUSL RE—Santa Maria Nuova Hospital	AUSL RE 5—SMN	Cardiologist	M	Manages the electrophysiology division of Santa Maria Nuova hospital (RE) and works as structured cardiologist	2005	Permanent
AUSL RE—Guastalla Hospital	AUSL RE 6—GUA	Emergency doctor	F	Works at the emergency room of Guastalla hospital (RE)	NA	Permanent
AUSL RE—Santa Maria Nuova Hospital	AUSL RE 7—SMN	Neurologist	M	Manages the neurology division of Santa Maria Nuova Hospital (RE) and works as structured neurologist	2017	Permanent
AUSL RE—Santa Maria Nuova Hospital	AUSL RE 8—SMN	IT specialist	M	Manages the medical equipment of Santa Maria Nuova Hospital (RE)	2006	Permanent
ASUR Marche—Riuniti Torrette Hospital	ASUR MARCHE 1	Emergency doctor	M	Manages planned and emergency medical transport of Riuniti Torrette hospital (AN)	1996	Permanent
ASUR Marche—Riuniti Torrette Hospital	ASUR MARCHE 2	Emergency doctor	F	Presence on both ambulances and air ambulances in the southern area of Ancona (AN)	2014	Temporary

(continued)

(continued)

Hospital	Interview code	Professional category	Sex	Main task	Company seniority (year of beginning)	Contract
ASUR Marche—Riuniti Torrette Hospital	ASUR MARCHE 3	Nurse	M	Works at the emergency room of Riuniti Torrette hospital (AN) and presence on the ambulances and *autoinfermieristiche* (nurse-staffed emergency vehicles)	2014	Permanent
ASUR Marche—Riuniti Torrette Hospital	ASUR MARCHE 4	Emergency doctor	F	Manages the emergency division of Riuniti Torrette hospital (AN) and works as structured emergency doctor	1998	Permanent
ASUR Marche—Riuniti Torrette Hospital	ASUR MARCHE 5	Nurse	F	Emergency room of Riuniti Torrette hospital (AN) and presence on both ambulances, *autoinfermieristich*e and air ambulances	2017	Permanent
ASUR Marche—Riuniti Torrette Hospital	ASUR MARCHE 6	Cardiologist	M	Manages the cardiac intensive care unit within the electrophysiology division of Riuniti Torrette hospital (AN) and works as structured cardiologist	2009	Permanent
ASUR Marche—Riuniti Torrette Hospital	ASUR MARCHE 7	Manager of emergency divisions	M	Manages the emergency division of ASUR Macerata (MC) and Ancona (AN)	2008	Permanent

REFERENCES

Agarwal, R., Guodong, G., DesRoches, C., & Jha, A. K. (2010). The digital transformation of healthcare: Current status and the road ahead. *Information Systems Research, 21*(4), 796–809. https://doi.org/10.1287/isre.1100.0327

Agenda Digitale, (2022). Sanità digitale: le tre priorità per il 2022. Retrieved April 29, 2024, from https://www.agendadigitale.eu/sanita/sanita-digitale-le-tre-priorita-per-il-2022

Alvesson, M., & Kärreman, D. (2011). Decolonializing discourse: Critical reflections on organizational discourse analysis. *Human relations, 64*(9), 1121–1146.

Autor, D. H., Levy, F., & Murnane, R. J. (2003). The skill content of recent technological change: An empirical exploration. *The Quarterly Journal of Economics, 118*(5), 1279–1333. https://doi.org/10.1162/003355303322552801

CERGAS – Centre for Research on Health and Social Care Management. (2017). Inquadramento economico del settore sanitario: la Lombardia nel confronto italiano ed europeo. OSPA Reports.

CREA Sanità. (2022). 19th Health Report. The (uncertain) future of the NHS, between macroeconomic compatibility and the urgency of reprogramming.

Consoli, D., & Mina, A. (2009). An evolutionary perspective on health innovation systems. *Journal of Evolutionary Economics, 19*, 297–319. https://doi.org/10.1007/s00191-008-0127-3

de Belvis, A. G., Meregaglia, M., Morsella, A., Adduci, A., Perilli, A., Cascini, F., Solipaca, A., Fattore, G., Ricciardi, W., Maresso, A., & Scarpetti, G. (2022). Italy: Health system review. *Health Systems in Transition, 24*(4), 1–236.

Dhanvijay, M. M., & Patil, S. C. (2019). Internet of Things: A survey of enabling technologies in healthcare and its applications. *Computer Networks, 153*, 113–131. https://doi.org/10.1016/j.comnet.2019.03.006

Donatini, A. (2020). The Italian health care system. In R. Tikkanen, R. Osborn, E. Mossialos, A. Djordjevic, & G. Wharton (Eds.), *International profiles of health care systems. The commonwealth fund*. Retrieved 7 October, 2024, from https://www.commonwealthfund.org/sites/default/files/2020-12/International_Profiles_of_Health_Care_Systems_Dec2020.pdf

Eden, R., Burton-Jones, A., Scott, I., Staib, A., & Sullivan, C. (2018). Effects of eHealth on hospital practice: Synthesis of the current literature. *Australian Health Review, 42*(5), 568–578. https://doi.org/10.1071/AH17255

Eurofound. (2020). Long-term care workforce: Employment and working conditions. Publications Office of the European Union. Retrieved April 29, 2024, from https://www.eurofound.europa.eu/publications/customised-report/2020/long-term-careworkforce-employment-and-working-conditions

EU-OSHA – European Agency for Safety and Health at Work. (2022a). Human health and social work activities – evidence from the European Survey of Enterprises on New and Emerging Risks. Retrieved April 29, 2024, from https://osha.europa.eu/en/publications/human-health-and-social-work-activities-evidence-european-survey-enterprises-new-and-emerging-risks-esener

EU-OSHA – European Agency for Safety and Health at Work. (2022b). Advanced robotics, artificial intelligence and the automation of tasks: definitions, uses, policies and strategies and Occupational Safety and Health. Retrieved April 29, 2024, from https://osha.europa.eu/en/publications/advanced-robotics-artificial-intelligence-and-automation-tasks-definitions-uses-policies-and-strategies-and-occupational-safety-and-health

Ferrera, M. (1995). Le quattro Europe sociali tra universalismo e selettività. *Giornale Di Diritto Del Lavoro E Di Relazioni Industriali*, 67.

Istat. (2020). *Annuario Statistico Italiano*.

Jaumotte, M. F., Li, L., Medici, A., Oikonomou, M., Pizzinelli, C., Shibata, M. I., & Tavares, M. M. (2023). Digitalization during the covid-19 crisis: Implications for productivity and labor markets in advanced economies. *International Monetary Fund*, 10(5089/9798400232596), 006.

Kissick, W. L. (1994). *Medicine's dilemmas: Infinite needs versus finite resources*. Yale University Press.

Kraus, S., Schiavone, F., Pluzhnikova, A., Invernizzi, A. C. (2021). Digital transformation in healthcare: Analyzing the current state-of-research. *Journal of Business Research*, 123, 557–567. https://doi.org/10.1016/j.jbusres.2020.10.030

Litwin, A. S. (2020). Technological change in health care delivery: Its drivers and consequences for work and workers. UC Berkeley Labor Center.

Litwin, A. S. (2022). Technological change on the frontlines of health care delivery. *Industrial and Labor Relations Review*, 75(4), 829–838.

Marques, I. C., & Ferreira, J. J. (2020). Digital transformation in the area of health: Systematic review of 45 years of evolution. *Health and Technology*, 10(3), 575–586. https://doi.org/10.1007/s12553-019-00402-8

Ministero della Salute. (2020). Indicazioni nazionali per l'erogazione di prestazioni in telemedicina. Retrieved April 29, 2024, from https://www.statoregioni.it/media/3221/p-3-csr-rep-n-215-17dic2020.pdf

Montobbio, F., Staccioli, F., Virgillito, M. E., & Vivarelli, M. (2022). Robots and the origin of their labour-saving impact. *Technological Forecasting and Social Change*, 174, 121–122. https://doi.org/10.1016/j.techfore.2021.121122

OECD, European Union,. (2022). Health at a glance: Europe 2022: State of health in the EU cycle. *OECD Publishing, Paris*,. https://doi.org/10.1787/507433b0-en

OECD. (2023). Ready for the Next Crisis? Investing in Health System Resilience, OECD Health Policy Studies, OECD Publishing, Paris.https://doi.org/10.1787/1e53cf80-en

Pavolini, E. (2020). La sanità italiana di fronte alla crisi del Coronavirus. Osservatorio Internazionale per la Coesione e l'Inclusione Sociale.

Pizzuti, F. R., Raitano, M., Tancioni, M. (2022). *Rapporto sullo stato sociale 2022: la crisi da Covid-19 e il welfare*. Sapienza University Press.

Presidenza del Consiglio dei Ministri. (2021). Piano nazionale di ripresa e resilienza. #nextgenerationitalia, Italia Domani. Retrieved April 29, 2024, from https://www.governo.it/sites/governo.it/files/PNRR.pdf

Rosenberg, N. (1994). *Exploring the black box: Technology, economics, and history*. Cambridge University Press. https://doi.org/10.1017/CBO9780511582554

Sanità Digitale. (2019). Sanità digitale: lo stato dell'arte. Retrieved April 29, 2024, from https://www.sanita-digitale.com/in-evidenza/sanita-digitale-lo-stato-dellarte/

Sostero, M. (2020). Automation and robots in services: review of data and taxonomy. JRC Technical Report.

Stoumpos, A. I., Kitsios, F., & Talias, M. A. (2023). Digital transformation in healthcare: technology acceptance and its applications. *International Journal of Environmental Research and Public Health, 20*(4), 34–07. https://doi.org/10.3390/ijerph20043407

Susskind, R., Susskind, D. (2015). *The future of the professions: How technology will transform the work of human experts.* Oxford University Press. https://doi.org/10.1093/oso/9780198713395.001.0001

Ufficio Parlamentare Bilancio. (2019). Focus n. 6 Lo stato della sanità in Italia. Rome: Parliamentary Budget Office. Retrieved April 29, 2024, from https://www.upbilancio.it/pubblicato-il-focus-n-6-lo-stato-della-sanita-in-italia

WHO. (2022). WHO Global Health Expenditure Database. Indicators and Data. Geneva: World Health Organization. Retrieved April 29, 2024, from https://apps.who.int/nha/database/ViewData/Indicators/en

Yin, R. K. (2014). *Case study research: Design and methods.* Sage Publications.

Zuboff, S. (1988). *In the age of the smart machine: The future of work and power.* Basic Books.

CHAPTER 4

Automation in Cleaning: Why Dirty, Invisible, and Risky Jobs Will Not Be Replaced by Robots Yet

Armanda Cetrulo, Caterina Manicardi, and Angelo Moro

Abstract This chapter aims to provide new qualitative evidence on the use of automated technologies in the cleaning industry, a sector characterized by gender and racial segregation and traversed by trends towards increased competitiveness and workforce flexibilization. With the emergence of multinational global players, a process of capital centralization coupled with the adoption of new models of work organization and labor management is underway. However, this sectoral reconfiguration has not resulted in concrete improvements in workers' material conditions, but rather in workload intensification and the weakening of workers' rights due to labor market deregulation and the spread of outsourcing practices. Looking at the adoption of new technologies, several interesting findings

A. Cetrulo (✉) · C. Manicardi
Institute of Economics, Sant'Anna School of Advanced Studies, Pisa, Italy
e-mail: armanda.cetrulo@santannapisa.it

A. Moro
University of Modena and Reggio Emilia, Modena, Italy

emerge, starting with the still limited diffusion of cleaning robots due to the unpredictability of physical environments, the crucial role played by manual dexterity, and the possibility for companies to rely on a flexible and low-paid workforce. Moreover, despite the high incidence of occupational hazards, health and safety issues are not significantly addressed when technological innovations are adopted. The data also highlights the weak role of unions, which are usually not involved in defining implementation strategies.

Keywords Cleaning · Automation · Invisible jobs · Case study

4.1 Introduction

The essential role of cleaners emerged from invisibility during the COVID-19 pandemic, a period in which ensuring clean and sanitized spaces for production and consumption was crucial for the functioning of the economic system (Eurofound, 2023; Guasti, 2020). Yet, five years after the explosion of the pandemic, their socio-economic and working conditions have not significantly improved, as the downsizing of public spending and the removal of emergency income support schemes further weakened their position (ILO, 2023). However, already before the COVID-19 health emergency, the cleaning sector was facing contradictory trends and reconfiguration dynamics in the spheres of market, labor, and institutional settings. This makes it an interesting case to observe how worsening working conditions and low wages—within the broader and structural dismantling of the Fordist regime—coupled with a pattern of capital centralization and growing adoption of new technologies (Aguiar & Herod, 2006).

In the last decades, the sector has indeed been experiencing both the effects of the progressive deregulation of labor market institutions (Baccaro & Howell, 2017), as evidenced by the wide adoption of outsourcing contracts for peripheral activities such as cleaning and security, and a push towards job "professionalization" through technological upgrading aimed at integrating digital and automated tools and raising the skill floor. These two trends produce a paradoxical outcome on labor, since instead of making these workers more visible and valuable, the professionalization and technological upgrading were adopted to make them as "silent" as possible (Aguiar & Herod, 2006). Similar patterns can be found in different sectors, but what is particularly interesting in the case of cleaning concerns first, the nature of the activity performed, usually conceived as a low-skilled one, belonging to the sphere of "menial" tasks, historically assigned to women and immigrant workers (Duffy, 2005; Glenn, 1992). Furthermore, the composition of the workforce highlights important sources of stratification, since gender and race segregation are usually accompanied by weak labor bargaining power (Folbre et al., 2023; ILO, 2023).

The aim of this chapter is to provide new qualitative evidence on how and to what degree the use of advanced technologies occurs in such a context, based on the assumption that the adoption of digital and automated innovations does not only respond to technical and productivity goals, but is shaped by hierarchical structures and power relations within and outside workplaces (Cetrulo & Nuvolari, 2019; Cirillo et al., 2021). The remainder of the chapter is organized as follows: we start by providing a general overview of the main challenges faced by cleaning workers in recent decades, both from an institutional, productive, and technological point of view. Then, after a brief presentation of the companies selected for the study, we illustrate the main findings emerging from the field research, where we identify drivers and barriers to adoption, together with the main impacts of cleaning robots and digital tools on labor. We conclude the chapter with some final remarks, addressing the potential role of social actors.

4.1.1 Setting the Scene

The cleaning sector is characterized by weak industrial relations (Larsen et al., 2022; Nizzoli, 2015; Tapia & Turner, 2013) and significant stratifications along class, gender, and race lines (Benelli, 2011; Bezuidenhout & Fakier, 2006). The workforce is predominantly composed of women, immigrants, and low-skilled workers who are typically engaged in labor-intensive tasks with minimal skill requirements (Eurofound, 2014). In the case of Italy, out of around 450 thousand workers employed in 2023 as janitors in offices, commercial services and ships, women represent 73% of the total workforce, while around 34% of new arrivals to the sector are immigrant workers (Istat). These dimensions add up to the very content of cleaning work, socially perceived as an innate female and also dirty activity because of the constant handling of trash and fluids (Hughes,

1962; Rabelo & Mahalingam, 2019). Such specific labor attributes translate into a structural "invisibility" of these workers both in the political and work sphere, in line with the systemic denial of the social reproductive sphere in a capitalistic system (Federici, 2021).

In fact, defining cleaning work as a low value-added activity has been functional to justify, even in the public debate, poor wages and harsh working conditions (Soni-Sinha & Yates, 2013). These jobs are indeed very badly remunerated and usually located in the lowest quartile of national wage distributions (Cetrulo et al., 2024; ILO, 2023). Moreover, labor market regulation has notably failed to address the major drawbacks of increasing outsourcing practices according to which non-core activities such as cleaning, have been progressively outsourced by public administrations and private companies, resulting in higher labor intensity, wage dumping and deterioration of physical and psychological conditions for outsourced workers (Mori, 2015).

As far as institutional barriers are concerned, the role of labor clauses in public procurement contracts should be mentioned. Labor clauses are intended to address the issues of low wages and precarious work in public supply chains and play different roles depending on each country's employment regime (Jaehrling et al., 2018). In Italy, these clauses, called "social clauses," are regulated by the Public Procurement Code of 2016 (later reformed in 2023) and are intended to promote the employment stability of personnel hired by contracting firms and the latter's application of sectoral collective agreements. However, according to Italian administrative jurisprudence, the adoption of social clauses in public tenders to safeguard employment stability must be interpreted elastically, without limiting the economic freedom of private operators or creating conflict with their own business organization. Consequently, social clauses in public procurement contracts are formulated in a flexible manner, allowing for leeway in the absorption of workers employed by the previous contractor (Dorigatti et al., 2024).

The market of cleaning services is indeed highly competitive, with user-firms typically selecting the lowest priced offer, forcing cleaning companies to squeeze their costs and shorten job contracts, as confirmed by the high incidence of non-standard employment in the sector. The prevalent use of part-time and temporary job contracts further augments the socio-economic vulnerability of these workers, who must accept flexible and uncertain working hours to preserve their wages (Ryan & Herod, 2006; Scandella, 2009). Unionization rates in the industrial cleaning sector are also low compared to the average unionization rate in the EU-28 countries (Eurofound, 2014). Nevertheless, in recent years and especially outside the EU, innovative mobilization tools were adopted, as shown by the US and Canada-based Janitors for Justice campaign (Tapia & Turner, 2013) and the creation of solidarity mechanisms among broader communities against outsourcing and subcontracting practices in the UK (Hughes & Woodcock, 2023; Pannini, 2023; Wills, 2008).

Concerning health and safety, cleaning labor represents one of the most dangerous occupations in terms of occupational hazards, since it records among the highest incidences of work-related injuries and musculoskeletal disorders (Charles et al., 2009).[1] Health risks are not simply due to the type of tasks performed (for instance, walking on a wet floor increases the risk of slippery), or exposure to chemical products, but also stem from different factors like the location and type of surfaces/materials to be cleaned (outside/inside, window/floor, etc.), the available facilities and work tools, and the environmental characteristics of workplaces. Indeed, cleaners work in a variety of sites, from hospitals to manufacturing industries or public gardens, each showing specific risks on thier own.

Moreover, given the need to guarantee clean spaces during opening hours (whether we refer to commercial sites, firms, hospitals, or schools), cleaners typically work alone or in small groups at night, in areas that are either too cold or too hot (because of the lack of air conditioning systems). Female workers are particularly impacted by night shifts, both because of the difficulties in carrying out care duties at home and because the risk of sexual harassment significantly increases during night, as recently document by the Uni Global Union.[2] More in general, constant isolation from other colleagues and frequent night shifts can feed a sense of invisibility that negatively affects workers' well-being (Bentein et al., 2017), causing emotional exhaustion and stress. The experience of workers reports that this feeling of invisibility is related both to the limited social interaction, but also to the content of the work itself, which is only recognized when not done properly (Rabelo & Mahalingam, 2019). At

---

[1] According to Schwartz et al. (2020, p. 837) '2.38 million janitors are employed in the U.S. and high physical workload may explain a lost-work days rate 2.7 times greater than other occupations.'

[2] The survey is available here: https://uniglobalunion.org/news/cleaners_survey_2023/ (retrieved on May 27th 2024).

the same time, invisibility seems to have been reinforced by work practices that leverage existing cultural ideologies and social stigma (Rabelo & Mahalingam, 2019; Simpson et al., 2012).[3] Moreover, janitors are not only subject to job-specific occupational hazards, but also to the ones peculiar to each workplace: in hospitals, they face higher infection risk, whereas in metal industries they are exposed to chemical risks and respiratory diseases (Salerno et al., 2012). To further worsen their health and safety conditions, cleaners often operate in spaces that were not designed for cleaning purposes, adding specific risks of logistic inadequacy to their occupational hazard (Zock, 2005).

In such a highly risky working environment, technological advancements have not necessarily addressed these issues. Rather than mitigating these risks, innovation seems to have essentially supported the adoption of work organization models based on increasing standardization and work intensity (Dochain & Nyssen, 2018). Indeed, the job of cleaners has been progressively transformed from a deskilled but varied and autonomous job into a highly repetitive and task-segmented one, leading to increased psychological stress (Aguiar, 2001). During the 80s, cleaning workers had more control over their daily tasks, deciding the order of their activities and their distribution across the different spaces. Part of this autonomy was also due to heterogeneities across workplaces, such that workers had to always adjust to different and unusual contexts, also modifying the set of tasks and protocols previously defined by their supervisors (Messing et al., 1992 as cited by Aguiar, 2001).

4.1.2 The Technological Dimension

Being a "dirty," repetitive, and dangerous occupation, the cleaning sector could virtually represent a favorable context for the introduction of robots or other automated technologies aimed at improving ergonomics, as usually advocated when discussing the benefits of human–robot collaboration in industry (Lorenzini et al., 2023). However, a plain adoption of these technologies has followed a quite discontinuous pattern in this sector. Following Schofield (1999), we can essentially describe a cleaning

---

[3] According to Hatton (2017), a job is made invisible in three cases: if its specific tasks are considered an innate property of individuals (as care work for women), if the work is performed remotely, or if it is carried out outside the boundaries of the law (i.e. sex work).

robot as a machine that moves on the area of interest without being guided, able to automatically perform specific operations such as changing the water flow or the pressure of the brush. Cleaning robots are equipped with sensors to identify obstacles and a programming interface defining the path and the process to be followed. Cleaning robots generally exist in two types, those for domestic use and those for professional use. The two categories differ greatly, both in terms of price and size, and in terms of performance and technological equipment.

Professional cleaning robots, on which we focus our attention, are in fact complex machines, often capable of operating several cleaning procedures at the same time (vacuum, spraying, scrubbing, drying, etc.) and equipped with sophisticated navigation and sensor systems and sometimes even quality control devices (Prassler et al., 2000). They were introduced during the 80s, even if already in the 70s Electrolux was conducting some trials on cleaning robot prototypes (Schofield, 1999). Robots of this first generation were generally only able to combine a few operations at the same time, although some prototypes, developed in the early 1990s, were already capable of scrubbing and vacuuming simultaneously. In addition, they were mostly equipped with ultrasonic sensors or infrared vision systems and were able to move either autonomously or along pre-programmed trajectories in teach-in mode (i.e., memorizing a manually executed trajectory) as well as by means of magnetic beacons placed on the ground (Prassler et al., 2000).

Among the first European applications worth recalling, there is the development, between the late 80s and the mid-90s, of the ST82 R VARIOTECH—an autonomous floor scrubber resulting from the collaboration between Hefter Cleantech and Siemens AG and implemented in supermarkets in Germany, Austria and the Netherlands, the airport of Manchester and an exhibition hall at EXPO 2000 (*ibid.*). Another cleaning robot able to climb over curbs and staircases—the CABX—was used in the same period in metro stations in France, being the result of a partnership between the public metro authority and several technology actors (*ibid.*).

Despite the high price and small series production, these early applications together with a fair amount of commercial availability of such systems raised expectations that professional cleaning robots would become increasingly common (*ibid.*). On the contrary, a survey conducted by the Worldwide Cleaning Industry Association ISSA in 2020 among manufacturers, technology providers and building service contractors across twelve European countries, revealed that even first-generation cleaning robots have not been as widely adopted as expected (DTO Research, ISSA, 2020). Also in those regions renowned for high levels of innovation in the industry, like Nordic European countries, cleaning robotics are still in a testing phase while digital tools are already widely in use. Among them, cleaning management software for real-time tracking of janitorial service schedules and immediate reporting to clients are more significantly diffused.[4]

In recent years, the development of cleaning robots has benefited from the wave of technological innovation known as Industry 4.0, mainly due to advances in sensor systems, connectivity and battery technology. Current models of cleaning robots are in fact able to autonomously generate surface maps thanks to laser scanners, working out the most efficient cleaning paths. They also tend to be connected via Wi-Fi or cellular data, thus being able to be managed remotely and provide real-time information of their performance. Battery life has been increased while recharging times have been decreased, allowing greater cost-effectiveness. Multifunctionality has been expanded, enabling combinations of different cleaning techniques in the same robot. Finally, artificial intelligence and machine learning techniques are being implemented in the latest models to refine the perception and navigation systems (Elkmann & Saenz, 2023).

To date, professional wet floor-scrubbing systems such as the Neo robot—developed by the Canadian company Avidbots—are, for example, widespread in several airports around the world (*ibid.*). However, in spite of these technological developments, professional cleaning robots are still far from being fully established on the market and experts tend to be much more cautious about deriving large-scale deployment from the mere commercial availability of technological solutions.

Although seemingly a simple task, automating an activity such as cleaning the floor in fact presents obstacles and difficulties. While industrial robots generally operate in controlled conditions (i.e., an enclosed work cell), performing pre-programmed sequences of elementary tasks, a

---

[4] There is also a growing interest in more sustainable cleaning solutions, ranging from pure water and dry products for surfaces disinfection, such as steam cleaners, electrostatic sprayers and UV light sanitizers, to research into bio-based cleaning agents able to reduce chemical dosing (DTO Research, ISSA, 2020; Kateeb, 2023).

cleaning robot operates instead in an open, often public and in most cases diverse environment. It must therefore be able to observe its surroundings and adapt its operations to possible, even unforeseen, changes in the environment (Prassler et al., 2000). Although recent advances in sensors and navigation systems have improved robots' capabilities, in many contexts they are still less efficient and flexible than human labor (Elkmann & Saenz, 2023). The relatively high cost of such technologies, coupled with their relative operational and maintenance complexity, completes the picture (ibid.).

However, recent developments in the market structure and the characteristics of the economic actors in the cleaning industry may provide drivers in the direction of more widespread automation. The market of facility management services, including both in-house and outsourced provision of either hard or soft facility management, has experienced a steady increase over the last thirty years, peaking at a market size of 1.291 USD trillion in 2024 (Mordor Intelligence, 2024). The concurrent rise of big players offering integrated services to end-users, observed in both the US and European markets, is attributed to several factors, including the increasing complexity of buildings and infrastructure, the standardization and bundling of simpler service tasks alongside a broader range of service and an expanding trend towards outsourcing of non-core activities for cost efficiency (Das Adhikari et al., 2019).

Several multinational actors and corporations active in the field are now increasing their market share globally (Kirov & Ramioul, 2014): the more competitive the market, the more professionalism and technological progress become strategic marketing tools to stand out from competitors (Aguiar & Herod, 2006). Among the most prominent actors, large business service contractors are in fact pushing for the adoption of new technologies, acting as preferential interlocutors for manufacturers, even if the rate of cooperative R&D is still at an infant stage. These contractors typically can dispose of substantial resources and manage the cleaning of large spaces such as malls, logistic centers and airports, which require a high number of staff for cleaning, encouraging the integration of technologies for cost reduction (DTO Research, ISSA, 2020).

As briefly anticipated before, the emergence of large market players is also driving the on-going adoption of new work organization models. More scientific and standardized methods of work inspired by lean principles and total quality management have been introduced to rationalize the entire process, starting from an overall assessment of the time needed to perform each operation to ensure an effective division of tasks, reduce costs and consequently increase productivity (Dochain & Nyssen, 2018). This miniaturization of work activity not only allows for more pervasive control, but also has the effect of making each worker more easily substitutable. In this sense, this extensive process of standardization, by making it possible to move from a set of multi-task work schedules to single-task individual performances, could favor the implementation of automation technologies.

At the same time, companies have engaged in a professional upgrading of the service provided, through an increasing adoption of international standards together with advanced technologies, within a restructuring process of the sector due to increasing international capital concentration and labor deregulation. However, while the occupational labels (and even the public discourse) are affected by this presumed upgrading with janitors becoming cleaning "specialists" or "technicians," their socioeconomic conditions are rather worsening in terms of salaries, work intensity, degree of autonomy and social vulnerability (Aguiar, 2006).

In summary, the cleaning industry offers an interesting perspective to study the process of adoption and implementation of automation technologies in the service sector, given the paradoxical trends that run through it. On the one hand, in fact, cleaning companies are radically exploiting the on-going deregulation of the labor markets to reduce labor costs and rely on an extremely flexible and precarious workforce. On the other hand, given the increasing competitiveness of the sector due to the proliferation of small actors within a process of capital centralization, companies are pushing towards professionalization and symbolic upgrading of these jobs, fostered by the adoption of advanced technologies and standardized work practices, without any improvement of workers' material conditions, but rather an intensification of the workload (Aguiar & Herod, 2006).

4.1.3 Methodology—A Workplace Analysis

As briefly mentioned above, professional cleaning robots can be used in a variety of workplaces, which tend to be characterized by the presence of large surfaces, such as airports, supermarkets, all kinds of halls or hallways (in factories, public buildings, metro stations, etc.). In addition, they can be adopted by firms operating in a wide range of sectors for the purpose of cleaning their premises, as well as firms providing specialized cleaning services. To identify a shortlist of potential adopters, several informal interviews were conducted with key stakeholders, industry experts, and major companies' representatives. Such a preliminary step was crucial for gaining insights, at the sectoral level, into both the state of technological adoption and its potential impacts. Finally, three workplaces were selected where cleaning robots have been adopted with greater or lesser success: an airport, a hospital and a manufacturing plant, all three located in Italy. In the first two cases, the robots were adopted by firms providing cleaning services, while in the last case, the company owning the factory directly adopted the device. Alongside this automated technology, we also paid attention to other forms of technological innovation occurring in these companies and especially to digitalization processes. Qualitative evidence in each site was collected through: (i) semi-structured interviews (both in presence and remotely) with workers, technicians and managers covering different occupational profiles; (ii) analysis of available documents; (iii) direct visits to the establishments, whenever feasible.

Among the three firms, the most comprehensive case of adoption and successful implementation of cleaning robots is represented by the Dussmann Service S.r.l.. The company is a division of the German Dussmann Group, that offers facility management and food services to hospitals, schools and universities, hotels, and transportation companies, and counts 66,000 employees operating in 21 countries. We specifically studied the adoption of such a robot at the Milan Malpensa airport, where Dussmann Service provides the cleaning service through a public procurement contract. Different job profiles were interviewed, from cleaning operators to IT specialists and managerial figures in the planning, control and innovation department, for a total of 6 interviews. Additional information was gathered through a field visit that made it possible to observe the technologies on-site. Moreover, also the innovation manager of the tech consulting firm providing the innovation plan to Dussmann Service was interviewed to get a better understanding of the process of development of new technological solutions. In fact, as will be explained in more detail later (par. 3.2), having realized that the technological solutions on the market were not suitable for their needs, in 2018 Dussmann Service turned to a technology consulting firm to find partners for developing and producing a customized autonomous cleaning robot. This firm first involved a university research center (the "E. Piaggio" center of the University of Pisa) and two robotics and industrial automation start-ups in the development of the prototypes and then identified a partner to industrialize the robot after acquiring the patent for the washing and navigation systems.

The second company included in the study is Coopservice, a cooperative society[5] based in Reggio Emilia (Emilia-Romagna), offering a wide array of services, including cleaning, security, warehouse logistics management, energy supply and plant maintenance. It belongs to the larger Coopservice Group, which oversees various subsidiaries operating in related sectors, with a total workforce of 25,500 employees, mostly operating in Italy. Coopservice was selected because of its significant role as a national provider of professional and healthcare cleaning services especially in the public sector. In this domain, the company makes extensive use of semi-automatic scrubber-dryers, and recently has also implemented autonomous cleaning robots, only to give up on them—as we shall see further on (par. 3.2)—due to technical difficulties inherent to the nature of the service and working environment. While finally abandoning the adoption of this specific technology, nevertheless the company implemented technological innovation processes, again mainly related to digitalization. We studied in particular the case of the hospital of Reggio Emilia, to which Coopservice provided the cleaning service at the time as part of a public procurement contract covering all the hospitals in the Emilia-Romagna region. In this case, 8 interviews were conducted, including the chief innovation and operating managers, IT specialists, HR managers, and a local trade union official from Filt-CGIL.

The third company, Nestlé Vera, stands as a direct adopter, having successfully integrated the technology into its production site in San Giorgio in Bosco, in the Veneto region. At the time of the fieldwork, two cleaning robots were operating in two separate aisles: one inside the production area and the other connecting the production area to the warehouse. The first robot was introduced in 2017 by the service company in charge of the warehouse cleaning, while the second was directly adopted by Nestlé Vera in the summer of 2021. The site of San Giorgio in Bosco, with approximately 200 employees,

---

[5] Widely spread in the service sector, cooperatives in Italy are characterized by very poor working conditions. Far from being a response to market pressures, these practices emerge as one of the key elements explaining the wide diffusion of this organization model, especially in the most labour-intensive sectors and especially among subcontracting actors (Dorigatti et al., 2024).

is dedicated to bottling water and soft drinks for restaurants, bars and large retailers. Production operations are regulated by a co-packaging agreement between the beverage packaging producer S.I.Con and Sanpellegrino S.p.A, one of the largest Italian manufacturers of water, soft drinks and related packaging, owned by the Swiss multinational company Nestlé. In this case, one single in-depth interview was conducted with the factory logistic manager at the site of San Giorgio in Bosco.

4.1.4 Findings

As described above, the three cases present interesting heterogeneity in terms of workplace context, degree of adoption and efficiency of new technological solutions, which could lead to different outcomes in terms of effective pervasiveness and labor impact of innovation. To better assess this variety, in this section we identify emerging similarities and differences, focusing on three main areas of interest, namely (i) drivers for the adoption of advanced cleaning tools, (ii) barriers to their implementation, and (iii) their impact on work organization and stakeholder involvement.

4.1.5 Drivers of Adoption

In analyzing the drivers leading to the adoption of automation cleaning technologies, the first distinction to be made is between the possibility of adoption and actual adoption. This distinction is necessary precisely due to the type of economic actors studied in this chapter. Two of them, in fact, Dussmann Service and Coopservice, are service providers—including cleaning services—and technology seems to play a specific role in increasing their competitiveness, irrespective of its concrete deployment. As the interviewees explain, when competing in public tenders, the availability of automation technologies, regardless of their future practical application, is likely to act as a competitive advantage with respect to other tenderers. These advantages not only translate into reputational effects that strengthen the company's position in the market, but can also contribute effectively in obtaining public contracts. Such alleged availability of automation technologies rarely translates into actual use, due to the numerous barriers to adoption that we will illustrate in a moment.

> We include such technologies in tender projects for marketing reasons and to be in line with competitors. The tender commission would take a rather

dim view of you not including cleaning machines in the project. [...] We are leaders in the sector, and we have to keep up with new technologies, especially because most of the time we deal with big clients in the industry that expect this kind of innovation.

Coopservice, IT Specialist[6]

Now we are the only one in the facilities management market with an automated cleaning machine that complies with high productivity standards. [...] This project gave us great visibility on the market and the hope is to foster Dussmann's reputation as a solid company able to offer innovative services to clients. [...] Also, the management of Milan Malpensa Airport is interested in the adoption and upgrading of the technology. We included it in the last proposal and now they are asking for feedback. They probably see it as a way to get advertising.

Dussmann Service, Head of the Planning, Control, and Innovation Department

There are, however, other and more traditional drivers pushing companies towards automation, starting from the goal of increasing productivity and reducing labor costs. The cases of Coopservice and Dussmann Service, while diverging in terms of outcome (the former resulting in a failed adoption and the latter being a case of successful implementation), provide similar findings on this point. For the management of both firms, the main incentive was the containment of labor costs through the reduction in working hours, especially during night shifts, which are more onerous than daily ones because of specific wage allowances. Nevertheless, this choice was not implying labor displacement, but rather a different distribution of tasks. Indeed, while exploiting cleaning robots to perform more easily automatable tasks, it was possible to reallocate operators to other tasks more difficult to automate. Furthermore, automated machines make it possible to optimize surface cleaning routes, reducing cleaning times and rationalizing resource consumption.

Night workers are costly and the main reason for integrating cleaning robots was the automation of the cleaning service on night shifts. In fact, with such a solution I can be sure that the route for cleaning is optimized

---

[6] The interview excerpts quoted in this section are partly reproduced from Cirillo et al., 2022.

> [...] that is something impossible to assess with ride-on cleaning machines. This also allows you to minimize the amount of detergent and correctly predict charging time. [...] Besides this, there is an additional advantage for the client since you avoid the invasiveness of the man-on-board machines passing near to people.

Coopservice, Chief Operating Officer

> The main objective remains to increase productivity. Given the constant increase in labor costs, we need to reduce working hours and, in order to achieve it, I need to mechanize cleaning services with low added value. [...] Operators should perform only those activities requiring human dexterity and precision such as cleaning toilets, keypads and handles. [...] We also expect to implement the technology in other structures: we are indeed discussing which hospitals and airports, among those where we have won contracts, could adopt the technology.

Dussmann Service, Head of the Planning, Control and Innovation Department

Nestlé Vera differs slightly from the two cases mentioned above, since here the project of technological upgrading was part of a more general process of automating the entire site, starting from the logistics and with several spill-over effects.

> I would not say that the cleaning robot is part of a comprehensive strategy of digital transformation for the plant, but we certainly had to reconsider the internal logistic fluxes and at that point it made sense to automate some cleaning activities as well. [...] Our provider of semi-automated solutions often came here to the San Giorgio plant [...] and started asking whether we would have been interested in experimenting with a robotized solution. [...] We wanted to automatize those activities with low value added and relocate the operator to more complex tasks. This is the main reason.

Nestlé Vera, Factory Logistic Manager

Looking more broadly at the nature of service provided, it also emerges from the interviews the need to achieve better tracking of both human and robot performance, and also, to improve communication and transparency with the customer. In both case studies involving service providers (Dussmann Service and Coopservice), automatic and semi-automatic machines are equipped with digital devices that allow the integration and communication of the machinery with the company's management system. As a result, machines can store and provide performance data and receive commands to guide navigation, such as maximum speed or tolerance to obstacles, or the extent of collisions before a preventive stop. Thanks to the possibility of tracking the performance enabled by digital tools, reporting to the customer also becomes faster and easier.

> In the public sector, the reporting process is often cumbersome. [...] If I set up a block-chain system that detects that I entered that room at 10 am, left at 10.30 am and the work program included half an hour of cleaning, then the service could be automatically considered carried out and this notification could be sent directly to the client. [...] This technology, irrespective of being integrated into autonomous or semi-autonomous cleaning machines, makes things transparent. We provide portals through which the customer can see the progress of the service but above all we share a process of reporting and certification of the service rendered.

Coopservice, Chief Operating Officer

4.1.6 *Barriers to Adoption*

The implementation process of autonomous cleaning robots followed different paths and, because of important barriers to a plain adoption, resulted in various and contrasting outcomes.

First, technical and environmental barriers are present in all three cases, but manifest themselves in different ways. In Coopservice, which attempted to introduce autonomous cleaning robots in a hospital, these barriers represented an insurmountable obstacle, which led both the company management and the customer (the hospital management) to agree to abandon the project. Indeed, the hospital represents a highly unstructured workplace that requires fine, precise, agile and fast intervention relying on dexterity and mobility, preventing the standardization—and thus the automation—of the cleaning service. Hospitals, moreover, are crowded with users, which hinders the continuous use of robots for safety reasons, as they were built in times when architectural barriers for robots were certainly not on the agenda.

> At conferences, at trade fairs, I note a lack of contact between the producer and whoever manages the service. There was great enthusiasm and then I asked them if they ever went to a hospital. That is, have you seen what

hospitals are like? [...] For instance, if there is a leakage of biological fluid I cannot tell the nurse to wait for the machine to come from the warehouse. [...] I have to remove it as soon as possible and only the operator is able to provide an immediate response.

Coopservice, Chief Operating Officer

A hospital works mainly with frightening access flows in the morning and then significantly reduces the activity in the afternoon. In common areas such as hospital lobbies where automatic solutions could be used today, the machine would stand still to protect the personnel. [...] There are also architectural constraints, in fact, the hospitals in Italy today date back to the 1960s...

Coopservice, Chief Innovation Officer

Similar barriers also emerged in the cases of Dussmann Service and Nestlé Vera, without however preventing the adoption of cleaning robots, but only limiting their implementation. For instance, in the case of the airport, environmental specific barriers were solved through specific organizational choices, namely limiting the use of cleaning robots to the central areas of the airport's wider surfaces (i.e., waiting rooms, corridors, etc.), while employing operators to clean the edges of these areas and perform those tasks requiring higher degree of dexterity (e.g., cleaning toilets or benches). Furthermore, also to restrict contacts with the public, robots were allocated exclusively to the night shift. In the Nestlé Vera case, the implementation of the cleaning robot was limited to an aisle with suitable surface characteristics. However, sensors allow the proximity of moving objects around the robot to be detected, enabling it to operate together with the plant employees.

In the past, operators using the scrubber-dryer cleaned both the edges and the center of surfaces. Today, they only dedicate themselves to the edges of the surface and other activities, which can be push-buttons, handles, toilets, dusting over floors, etc. [...] [The robot] could also work during the day, but amid people it would get stuck all the time so it would not be used properly. Up to a certain time at night the airport has a big presence, but from 1.30-2 am the machine can work well.

Dussmann Service, IT Specialist

We went to adopt this machine here in an area that is practically a long aisle between our automatic warehouse and the end of the production line. This area here is practically an area that lends itself well to this type of robot because it is a fairly flat area and therefore does not have any particular problems. [...] After that, we use it practically every day except Saturdays and Sundays [...] and if there are people walking or even forklifts, because these robots operate at a walking speed, in short, they don't create any problems, let's say for safety and traffic. [...] Fortunately, it is not susceptible to the presence of people and it keeps moving.

Nestlé Vera, Factory Logistic Manager

Apart from technological and environmental barriers, other obstacles arose from financial and institutional constraints. The huge cost of such technological innovation was an issue faced especially in the case of Dussmann Service, leading the company to develop its own customized cleaning robot jointly with a university research center. The opportunity to benefit from public subsidies linked to the national Industry 4.0 Plan[7] helped to meet central management reluctance to an investment that nevertheless remained quite huge (an initial investment of €140,000 and a further €260,000 to bring the robot up to its full potential).

> The machines that are on the market today did not meet our needs, and so we started the project to work on specifications [...] that would be functional for those who work in the facility sector, i.e., to have a highly productive machine with low costs, easy to program, versatile, with certain dimensions and characteristics. [...] The biggest difficulty was mine in convincing the top management of Dussmann to do this kind of project.

---

[7] The *Piano Nazionale Industria 4.0* was an industrial policy launched by the Italian government in 2016 to promote the digitalisation of Italian companies. It consisted of a series of policies, mostly fiscal in nature, aimed at encouraging investments in research and development and technology. One of the tools used by this plan was the tax credit on R&D expenditure, which allowed companies that increased their R&D costs in the 2017–2020 period to recover their investments up to 50 per cent in tax reduction. The measure applied to expenditure on fundamental research, industrial research, and experimental development (including personnel costs, research contracts with other entities) and industrial patents. See:https://indd.adobe.com/view/00d6d24f-5dcc-41ea-831f%204dd4f50d5e74.

Dussmann Service, Head of the Planning, Control and Innovation Department

Other barriers relate to the institutional and social domain, as they concern possible consequences of new technologies in terms of job losses or adverse repercussions on employees. In theory, companies working in public procurement for labor-intensive services might be discouraged from investing in automation technologies if they are bound to preserve employment levels, due to the presence of "social clauses." However according to the interviewees, these clauses are only a partial constraint on the adoption of automation technologies. This depends both on the limited labor-saving effect of robots in the short term (since they require monitoring and maintenance, as we will see in the next section), and on the flexibility allowed by social clauses in managing potential labor displacement in the medium term:

> The fact that you have to consider is that, for example, in a large contract you have 100 people, and of these 100 people there is also a physiological turnover. So if I don't hire any more people, at the end of the three years of the contract, of these 100 I might have 90. If a normal scrubber-dryer costs me 15,000 euros, a self-operating scrubber-dryer costs me 25,000 euros, so I'm not upset about introducing a few self-operating scrubber-dryers.[...] I don't have such a devastating impact to say that the social clause stops me from doing that.

Coopservice, Chief Operating Officer

4.1.7 Labor Impact and the Role of Trade Unions

When looking at the labor impact of new technologies, a first issue concerns workers' responses to the adoption of automation technologies. Interestingly, in all cases, managers' fear about the adverse reaction of workers to new technologies turned out to be much bigger than workers' real concerns. The introduction of the autonomous cleaning robot in the Dussmann Service case provides a useful example of such a dynamic: on the one hand, the management opts for a gradual introduction of the new technology to prevent negative reactions, on the other hand, the workers do not seem to express excessive concerns about the occupational impact, but rather show a certain satisfaction about observed improvements.

It's something that goes by stages because we can't come to a tender and say 'Look, from tomorrow I'm going to put this machine in and your 8 hours become 4.' Because an insurrection comes out. [...] Now the process is to introduce the machine to the operators, because clearly they have never seen it, there is an important learning curve. And then you have to reorganize the work and that is what we are doing to get the benefit.

Dussmann Service, Head of the Planning, Control and Innovation Department

> There have been some colleagues who have said 'You see, they've taken the machines now they're going to fire us,' but I don't have that fear. It's like when the computer was born. Also because the machine doesn't clean a corner, it doesn't do the sanitation, it doesn't clean under the seat. So I say again – it may be that I'm not yet familiar with the machine so I'll answer you this way – but it's a great machine, they'll probably put it in during the day despite the obstacles.'

Dussmann Service, Cleaning Operator

The introduction of new technologies is also associated with the implementation of training initiatives. Internal training, however, seems to be intended more for intermediate figures than for operators, as the final goal is to promote the development of technological and managerial "soft" skills. This is the case, for instance, of Coopservice, which has set up a training program called 'Coopservice way', directed especially to the contract leaders, each of whom is responsible for the overall management of a specific site, and the team leaders, who coordinate and supervise groups of operators. In management's intentions, this program should also contribute to a better social acceptance of new technologies among employees, with team leaders playing the role of facilitators.

> What is happening is that contract leaders, who used to be adequate, today are struggling to keep up with the times. That's why we set up the Coopservice way, to try to convert them and integrate skills. [...] It is an internal training program for current employees to try to convert or professionalize the people we already have and it is an almost continuous training program, almost like an academy that alternates soft skills, i.e. programming, team building, etc., with courses on technical skills such as labor regulations, technology, IT, compliance, etc.

Coopservice, Chief Operating Officer

> Every time there is something new, operators show some kind of resistance. [...] Team leaders are the ones to foster to avoid these problems. If they know how the machine works and its potential, and if they are convinced, the enthusiasm within the whole team of operators would follow.

Coopservice, Development and Training Manager

On the contrary, no evidence was found of a similar learning trend for operators. In the case of Dussmann Service, for example, the operators working on the new cleaning robot only received brief on-the-job instructions on the use of the machine. The interface of the latter, in the design phase, was simplified specifically to make it immediately accessible to operators with basic digital skills. Operators working with the robot were selected according to their degree of familiarity with basic digital technologies such as smartphones, touchpads, etc. Furthermore, male colleagues perceive female workers as generally lacking familiarity with digital technologies. Thus, a certain digital gender divide seems to emerge both because women tend to avoid night shifts (during which these technologies are more widely used) and because they are deemed as less skilled in terms of digital competences with respect to their male counterparts.

> We kept the machine easy to use, with a friendly user interface and no complex installation procedures. Another weakness in existing solutions is that they require a skilled final user, who most of the time you cannot really afford.

Dussmann Service, Head of the Planning, Control and Innovation Department

> The selection criterion was the supposed familiarity with digital technologies among those workers operating during night shifts. [...] So they chose those who were already at ease with monitors, touchscreen and so on.

Dussmann Service, Cleaning Operator

> When the new machine arrived, they used to rotate workers for the night shift, but [...] there were female workers with families who complained about the rotation system [...] and now there are 20-25 people working

voluntarily at night on a permanent basis. [...] With the rotating night shift, it was possible that even women had to operate the machine [...] but they generally lacked a bit of digital skill [...] so it is better now.

Dussmann Service, Cleaning Operator

Concerning work organization, interesting evidence emerges from the Dussmann Service case. Here, the adoption of the new cleaning robot does not seem to have impacted on working pace, leaving to workers a relative autonomy in setting procedures.[8] Plus, despite the cleaning robot allowing for data storage along the entire process, these data are used, so far, only for technical improvements rather than to track workers' performance.[9] However, more significant changes were observed in the distribution of tasks. In fact, the operators have experienced an increase in the number and type of tasks they have to perform as, while continuing to carry out their ordinary cleaning duties, they have to deal with the activation, control, and maintenance of the robot.

Just to give an idea, when starting her shift, the operator places the robot on the marker of the corresponding cleaning cell[10] and then launches the cleaning program. While the machine is working, the operator keeps an eye on it and carries out other tasks such as emptying waste bins, cleaning the bathrooms, and removing dust from chairs. Since the robot is kept several inches away from the walls, the operator has to eventually clean those unserviced areas. At the end of the shift, a short report on the use of the machine and its functioning is required. Moreover, the use of the cleaning robot also demands daily intervention by the operator to refill the water and the detergent, drain the dirty water, clean the filter and change it at the end of the activity. Interestingly, this process of task densification is perceived as stressful by some operators, mostly because of the high cost of the robot and the control responsibilities involved.

---

[8] In fact, as for semi-automated solutions, autonomous artefacts need to be activated manually by workers according to Directive 2006/42/EC

[9] A similar conclusion can be drawn for Coopservice, which uses data collected by semi-automated solutions in the field to automatize the reporting process to the client rather than monitoring operators' behavior.

[10] The maps of the areas to cover are embedded in the software of the machine and divided into cells. Each cell has a starting point marked by a sticker on the floor. Correct positioning is crucial since the navigation system counts the meters travelled to assess the completion of a cell instead of relying on geolocation.

As the night shift starts I go to the warehouse, touch the screen on the machine and unblock it. Then I move it to the sticker and launch the cleaning program. In the meantime you possibly pay attention to the machine at work, you watch over it, and then take the other [semi-automated] washer dryer; it happens to work in parallel. [...] If it freezes, you can unblock the wheels manually and bring it back to the deposit. Of course, you report it to the shift manager and the following morning you write the report. At the end of the shift you flush the waste water and clean the suction tube, since the dirt dries out if you just leave it. Actually, it is not really different from old [semi-automated] machines, since we do this kind of daily maintenance for them too [...] nor did it change the effort we made in cleaning operations [...] cleaning the floor was something which we were already using the scrubber-dryer for, it was not done manually. [...] Now we use the joystick to move the machine.

Dussmann Service, Cleaning Operator

Actually you cannot leave the machine alone: you always have to keep an eye on it during work since the airport is open, even during the night. You can do other tasks in the meantime, but it is safer not to lose sight of it. [...] The machine is costly, and I am afraid when I have to use it during the shift. [...] It is a great responsibility for us, and this is certainly something new.

Dussmann Service, Cleaning Operator

Finally, our interviews also revealed an extremely low and limited involvement of trade unions in the technological choices made by both tendering authorities and contractors. This situation is the result both of structural conditions—fragmentation of the service, limited time horizon—and of agentive factors related to the managerial culture and trade union's urgency to negotiate on working conditions. At the same time, the coupling of a low wage and highly flexible workforce with widespread outsourcing strategies seem to hinder "positive" technological innovation (in terms of ergonomic enhancement):

Question: Notwithstanding the fact that the technology of the automatic cleaner was not adopted in the end, however was its introduction, adoption and implementation discussed with you, let's say?
[...] If I were to tell you, have we ever discussed these things here? Absolutely not. [...] In the trade union meetings that we have also had with Coopservice [...] the issue of health and safety is an issue that is addressed.

I think about the subject of the exoskeleton [...] to reduce fatigue and effort. It is true, however, that this is a technology that has a cost that is hardly bearable in a cleaning contract, while what could also be the potential to safeguard the health of these people is not fully grasped, because these are workers for whom the biological clock is obviously ticking and doing heavy manual work they have a reduced working capacity. And sometimes the discussion is not intercepted upstream of the problem but downstream, i.e. how I can then relocate this person within the company, and this discussion becomes increasingly complicated because there are many people with reduced working capacity and you obviously no longer have the jobs [that you can assign to them], unless you make technical organizational interventions or you discuss with the client the work that is contracted out.

Filt-Cgil, Union Official

4.1.8 Concluding Remarks and Future Challenges for Social Actors

Several interesting findings emerge from these case studies. First, the implementation and diffusion of automated technologies appears still limited, while digital tools are progressively integrated along the entire process. Indeed, projects of full automation of cleaning activities are hampered by several obstacles, related to the high degree of manual dexterity needed for specific tasks, the workspace adequacy for the circulation of cleaning robots and the relatively huge costs of investment. Once implemented, the labor-saving effect of these technologies seems to be very limited in the short term, since, at least until full operational autonomy is achieved, the robot needs to be constantly monitored by operators. Nevertheless, the managerial aim is also to take advantage of the potential labor-savings impacts of these technologies in the medium term. Given the increasing competition in the sector and the emergence of big transnational companies providing this type of service, the availability of advanced technological solutions acts as an important competitive leverage to affirm the "professionalized" nature of the service provided. However, these investments are not accompanied by a process of re/up-skilling of operators, though, for instance, the provision of training courses. At the same time, operators are invested with new responsibilities and maintenance tasks that increase the work intensity and related stress.

Moreover, despite the high incidence of occupational hazards and environmental workplace risks in the cleaning sector, health and safety issues are not significantly addressed when discussing technological innovations. This represents an interesting finding—that could be better explored in the future—in contrast to what emerges in the manufacturing sector where, on the contrary, ergonomic goals are usually presented as one of the main drivers of technological upgrading also to gain workers consent and greater legitimacy (Garibaldo & Rinaldini (eds.), 2022).

With respect to the direct involvement of social actors, the evidence collected confirms the weak role played by unions, which are neither informed about investment plans in new technologies nor involved in defining the implementation strategies. This evidence clearly reflects a more structural weakness of social actors in exercising their functions in a context characterized by labor fragmentation and loose institutional constraints.

Particularly in the public sector, a greater involvement of trade unions, right from the tender preparation stage, would be crucial to promote better working conditions and steer the adoption of new technologies in the right direction. However, while the literature reports virtuous cases of local experiments of unions negotiating stricter protocols for working conditions in public procurement, the reality remains that of an insufficient regulatory framework to guarantee workers' protection and of scarce public resources that favor downward competition (Pais & Mori, 2023; Pedaci & Di Federico, 2016). Such reality is likely to be even harsher in private outsourcing (Drahokoupil, 2015).

In this case, the development of more "inclusive" bargaining aimed at empowering all workers located in the same site despite being hired by different employers (Cetrulo & Moro, 2022), could help to improve working conditions and also shape the dynamics of technological innovation with important spill-over effects. More generally, beyond ensuring workers' individual protection in such a fragmented and invisible sector (Nizzoli, 2015), unions would benefit from increasing their efforts to organize and mobilize workers (Tapia & Turner, 2013). The recent mobilizations in the health and social care sector during the Covid pandemic in Italy (Galanti, 2022) and worldwide (Pelling, 2022) prove that such efforts can be effective, even if major institutional changes are necessary to make them permanent, starting from devoting more attention to this category of workers. Indeed, exploring the impact of new technologies on cleaners can contribute to shed light on marginalized but essential activities that are de facto widespread in all workplaces, despite socio-institutional attempts to keep these workers "out of sight."

APPENDIX

Case	Profession	Age	Sex	Main task	Company seniority	Type of contract	Union membership	Interview date	Interview duration
Dussmann Service S.r.l	Team Leader Cleaning Operator	60	M	Cleaning activity at the airport during night shifts and supervision of a cleaning unit	2016	Permanent (third-level operator)	Yes	7.01.2022	33'
Dussmann Service S.r.l	Head of Planning, Control and Innovation Department	42	M	Management of the Planning, Control and Innovation Department of Dussmann Service S.r.l	2014	Permanent	No	7.01.2022	37'
Dussmann Service S.r.l	IT Specialist	NA	M	Technical management of cleaning machines of Dussmann Service S.r.l	2018	Permanent	NA	7.01.2022	44'
Dussmann Service S.r.l	Cleaning Operator	57	M	Cleaning activity during day shifts	2015	Permanent (second-level operator)	Yes	7.01.2022	22'
Dussmann Service S.r.l	Head of Cleaning Service for the external area of Malpensa Airport (Site Manager)	NA	M	Management and supervision of the cleaning unit for the external area of Malpensa Airport	1998	Permanent	Yes	7.01.2022	53'
Dussmann Service S.r.l	Cleaning Operator	52	M	Cleaning activity during night shifts	2014	Permanent	NA	7.01.2022	32'

(continued)

(continued)

Case	Profession	Age	Sex	Main task	Company seniority	Type of contract	Union membership	Interview date	Interview duration
Dussmann Service S.r.l	Innovation Manager of Warrant Innovation Lab S.r.l	NA	F	Support of innovation projects including conceptualization, search for industrial partners and project implementation	2017	Permanent	NA	4.02.2022	27'
Coopservice	Chief Innovation Officer	51	M	Management of a technical unit dedicated to the conceptualization of innovative projects	2001	Permanent	NA	17.11.2021	53'
Coopservice	Chief Operating Officer	NA	M	Management of the operational phase after the award of a tender	2018	Permanent	NA	17.11.2021	47'
Coopservice	IT Specialist	41	M	Coordination of the "soft" and "soft-security" services for cleaning and logistic tenders within the IT Department	2019	Permanent	NA	17.11.2021	46'
Coopservice	IT Specialist	41	M	Management of the IT Department	2019	Permanent	NA	17.11.2021	53'
Coopservice	HR Manager	NA	M	Management of the recruitment and selection process	2018	Permanent	No	17.11.2021	28'

(continued)

(continued)

Case	Profession	Age	Sex	Main task	Company seniority	Type of contract	Union membership	Interview date	Interview duration
Coopservice	IT Specialist	NA	M	Development of software solutions for semi-automated cleaning machines	NA	Permanent	NA	17.11.2021	44'
Coopservice	Union Official of Filt-CGIL	NA	M	Protection of workers' rights in the logistics sector	NA	Permanent	Yes	17.11.2021	50'
Coopservice	Coordinator of Employee Training and Development within the HR Department	NA	F	Organization of technical training courses and provision of general career services	1998	Permanent	No	17.11.2021	36'
Nestlé Vera	Factory Logistic Manager for the San Giorgio in Bosco plant	NA	F	Management of logistics process automation projects in two San Pellegrino S.p.A. plants	2014	Permanent	No	4.11.2021	48'

References

Aguiar, L. L. (2001). Doing cleaning work "scientifically": The reorganization of work in the contract building cleaning industry. *Economic and Industry Democracy, 22*(2), 239–270. https://doi.org/10.1177/0143831X0122200

Aguiar, L. L. (2006). Janitors and sweatshop citizenship in Canada. *Antipode, 38*(3), 440–461. https://doi.org/10.1111/j.0066-4812.2006.00589.x

Aguiar, L. L., & Herod, A. (Eds.). (2006). *The dirty work of neoliberalism: Cleaners in the global economy*. Blackwell Publishing. ISBN: 9781405156363.

Baccaro, L., & Howell, C. (2017). *Trajectories of neoliberal transformation: European industrial relations since the 1970s*. Cambridge University Press. https://doi.org/10.1017/9781139088381

Benelli, N. (2011). Sweeping the streets of the neoliberal city: Racial and class divisions among New York City. *Journal of Workplace Rights, 16*(3–4), 453–474. https://doi.org/10.2190/WR.16.3-4.l

Bentein, K., Garcia, A., Guerrero, S., & Herrbach, O. (2017). How does social isolation in a context of dirty work increase emotional exhaustion and inhibit work engagement? A Process Model. *Personnel Review, 46*(8), 1620–1634. https://doi.org/10.1108/PR-09-2016-0227

Bezuidenhout, A., & Fakier, K. (2006). Maria's burden: Contract cleaning and the crisis of social reproduction in post-apartheid South Africa. *Antipode, 38*(3), 462–485. https://doi.org/10.1111/j.0066-4812.2006.00590.x

Cetrulo, A., & Nuvolari, A. (2019). Industry 4.0: Revolution or hype? Reassessing recent technological trends and their impact on labour. *Journal of Industrial and Business Economics, 46*, 391–402. https://doi.org/10.1007/s40812-019-00132-y

Cetrulo, A., & Moro, A. (2022). Una contrattazione alla Bolognese? Relazioni industriali e negoziazione aziendale nel settore metalmeccanico a Bologna dall'autunno caldo ad oggi. In F. Garibaldo & M. Rinaldini (Eds.), *Il lavoro operaio digitalizzato: inchiesta nell'industria metalmeccanica bolognese* (pp. 93–119). Bologna: Il Mulino. ISBN: 978-88-15-29523-1.

Cetrulo, A., Guarascio, D., Virgillito, M. E. (2024). Two neglected origins of inequality: hierarchical power and care work (No. 2024/04). Laboratory of Economics and Management (LEM), Sant'Anna School of Advanced Studies, Pisa, Italy, ISSN (Online): 2284–0400.

Cirillo, V., Rinaldini, M., Staccioli, J., & Virgillito, M. E. (2021). Technology vs. workers: The case of Italy's Industry 4.0 factories. *Structural Change and Economic Dynamics, 56*, 166–183. https://doi.org/10.1016/j.strueco.2020.09.007

Cirillo, V., Rinaldini, M., Virgillito, M. E., Divella, M., Manicardi, C., Massimo, F. S., Cetrulo, A., Costantini, E., Moro, A., & Staccioli, J. (2022). Case studies of automation in services. Luxembourg: Publications Office of the

European Union, chapter 4 "Professional cleaning robots" (pp. 41–59). https://doi.org/10.2760/347087

Charles, L. E., Loomis, D., & Demissie, Z. (2009). Occupational hazards experienced by cleaning workers and janitors: A review of the epidemiologic literature. *Work, 34*(1), 105–116. https://doi.org/10.3233/WOR-2009-0907

Das Adhikari, E., Hoffman, S., & Lietke, B. (2019). *Six emerging trends in facilities management sourcing*. McKinsey and Company. Retrieved December 16, 2024, from https://www.mckinsey.com/capabilities/operations/our-insights/six-emerging-trends-in-facilities-management-sourcing/

Dochain, M., & Nyssen, A. S. (2018). The Lean paradox: Does applying Lean Management increase protocol deviations? A case study of cleaning staff in the hospital sector. *International Journal of Healthcare Management, 13*(sup1), 311–317. https://doi.org/10.1080/20479700.2018.1540185

Dorigatti, L., Iannuzzi, F. E., Piro, V., & Sacchetto, D. (2024). Job quality in worker cooperatives: Beyond degeneration and intrinsic rewards. *British Journal of Industrial Relations, 62*, 591–613. https://doi.org/10.1111/bjir.12798

Drahokoupil, J. (Ed.). (2015). *The outsourcing challenge: Organizing workers across fragmented production networks*. ETUI. ISBN: 978-2-87452-366-3.

DTO Research, ISSA. (2020). How the cleaning industry is approaching innovation: Facts, trends and outlook for Europe. White Paper 2020. Retrieved December 16, 2024, from https://www.fm-house.com/wp-content/uploads/2020/11/How-the-Cleaning-Industry-is-approaching-Innovation-Facts-Trends-and-Outlook-for-Europe.pdf

Duffy, M. (2005). Reproducing labor inequalities: Challenges for feminists conceptualizing care at the intersections of gender, race, and class. *Gender & Society, 19*(1), 66–8. https://doi.org/10.1177/0891243204269499

Elkmann, N., & Saenz, J. (2023). Cleaning automation. In S. Y. Nof (Ed.), *Springer Handbook of Automation* (pp. 1159–1169). Springer. https://doi.org/10.1007/978-3-030-96729-1_53

Eurofound. (2014). *Industrial cleaning: Working conditions and job quality*. Eurofound. Retrieved December 16, 2024, from https://www.eurofound.europa.eu/en/publications/2014/industrial-cleaning-working-conditions-and-job-quality

Eurofound. (2023), *Job quality of COVID-19 pandemic essential workers, European Working Conditions Telephone Survey series*. Luxembourg: Publications Office of the European Union. Retrieved December 16, 2024, from https://www.eurofound.europa.eu/en/publications/2023/job-quality-covid-19-pandemic-essential-workers

Federici, S. (2021). *Patriarchy of the wage: Notes on Marx, gender, and feminism*. PM Press. ISBN: 9781629637990/9781629638584.

Folbre, N., Gautham, L., & Smith, K. (2023). Gender inequality, bargaining, and pay in care services in the United States. *ILR Review, 76*(1), 86–111. https://doi.org/10.1177/00197939221091157

Galanti, C. (2022). National heroes, disposable workers. How collective action in the health and social care sector during the pandemic negotiated with the self-sacrificing worker ideal. *Gender, Work & Organization, 31*(2), 606–624. https://doi.org/10.1111/gwao.12852

Garibaldo, F., & Rinaldini, M. (Eds.). (2022). *Il lavoro operaio digitalizzato. Inchiesta nell'industria metalmeccanica bolognese*. Il Mulino, ISBN: 978-88-15-29523-1.

Glenn, E. N. (1992). From servitude to service work: Historical continuities in the racial division of paid reproductive labor. *Signs: Journal of Women in Culture and Society, 18*(1), 1–43. https://doi.org/10.1086/494777

Guasti, N. (2020). The plight of essential workers during the COVID-19 pandemic. *Lancet, 395*(10237), 1587. https://doi.org/10.1016/S0140-6736(20)31200-9

Hughes, E. (1962). Good People and Dirty Work. *Social Problems, 10*(1), 3–11. https://doi.org/10.2307/799402

Hatton, E. (2017). Mechanisms of invisibility: Rethinking the concept of invisible work. *Work, Employment and Society, 31*(2), 336–351. https://doi.org/10.1177/0950017016674894

Hughes, L., & Woodcock, J. (2023). *Troublemaking: Why you should organize your workplace*. Verso Books. ISBN: 9781839767104.

ILO. (2023). *Work employment and social outlook 2023: The value of essential work*. Geneva: International Labour Office, ISBN: 9789220366516.

Jaehrling, K., Johnson, M., Larsen, T. P., Refslund, B., & Grimshaw, D. (2018). Tackling precarious work in public supply chains: A comparison of local government procurement policies in Denmark, Germany and the UK. *Work, Employment & Society, 32*(3), 546–563. https://doi.org/10.1177/0950017018758216

Kirov, V., & Ramioul, M. (2014). Quality of work in the cleaning industry: A complex picture based on sectoral regulation and customer-driven conditions. In M. Hauptmeier & M. Vidal (Eds.), *The comparative political economy of work* (pp. 290–311). London: Bloomsbury Publishing. https://doi.org/10.1007/978-1-137-32228-9_14

Larsen, T. P., Mailand, M., & Schulten, T. (2022). Good intentions meet harsh realities: Social dialogue and precarious work in industrial cleaning. *Economic and Industrial Democracy, 43*(1), 7–31. https://doi.org/10.1177/0143831X19880265

Lorenzini, M., Lagomarsino, M., Fortini, L., Gholami, S., & Ajoudani, A. (2023). Ergonomic human-robot collaboration in industry: A review. *Frontiers in Robotics and AI, 9*, 813907. https://doi.org/10.3389/frobt.2022.813907

Messing, K., Haentjens, C., & Doniol-Shaw, G. (1992). L'Invisible Nécessaire: l'activité de nettoyage de toilettes sur le trains de voyageurs en gare. *Le Travail Humain, 55*(4), 353–370.

Mordor Intelligence. (2024). Facility management market size & share analysis—Growth trends & forecasts (2024–2029). Retrieved 27 April, 2024, from https://www.mordorintelligence.com/industry-reports/facility-management-market

Mori, A. (2015). Outsourcing public services: Local government in Italy, England and Denmark. In J. Drahokoupil (Ed.), *The outsourcing challenge: organizing workers across fragmented production networks* (pp. 137–155). Brussels: ETUI. ISBN: 9782874523663.

Nizzoli, C. (2015). *C'est du propre ! Syndicalisme et travailleurs du « bas de l'échelle » (Marseille et Bologne)*. Presses universitaires de France. ISBN: 9782130635307.

Pais, I., & Mori, A. (2023). Towards new forms of economic and political action: From voice to entry. In S. P. de Guzmán, M. Iglesias-Onofrio, & I. Pais (Eds.), *Contingent workers' voice in Southern Europe: Collective experiences of protection and representation* (pp. 177–196). Elgar. https://doi.org/10.4337/9781802205572.00020

Pannini, E. (2023). Winning a battle against the odds: A cleaners' campaign. *Economic and Industrial Democracy, 44*(1), 68–87. https://doi.org/10.1177/0143831X211060390

Pedaci, M., & Di Federico, R. (2016). Outsourcing e precarietà del lavoro. Uno studio sul settore dei servizi di pulizia. *Quaderni di Rassegna Sindacale - Lavori, 27*(4), 103–121.

Pelling, L. (2022). Post-pandemic Hopes and Disappointments. Friedrich-Ebert-Stiftung—Politics for Europe. Retrieved December 16, 2024, from https://library.fes.de/pdf-files/bueros/stockholm/20159.pdf

Prassler, E., Ritter, A., Schaeffer, C., & Fiorini, P. (2000). A short history of cleaning robots. *Autonomous Robots, 9*, 211–226. https://doi.org/10.1023/A:1008974515925

Rabelo, V. C., & Mahalingam, R. (2019). "They really don't want to see us": How cleaners experience invisible 'dirty' work. *Journal of Vocational Behavior, 113*, 103–114. https://doi.org/10.1016/j.jvb.2018.10.010

Ryan, S., & Herod, A. (2006). Restructuring the architecture of state regulation in the Australian and Aotearoa/New Zealand cleaning industries and the growth of precarious employment. *Antipode, 38*(3), 486–507. https://doi.org/10.1111/j.0066-4812.2006.00591.x

Salerno, S., Kolman, V., Livigni, L., Magrini, A., Bosco, M. G., & Talamanca, I. F. (2012). Women's working conditions in hospital cleaning: A case study. *Work, 41*(Supplement 1), 4315–4319. https://doi.org/10.3233/WOR-2012-0726-4315

Scandella, F. (2009). Travail invisible dans un secteur de relégation: La double condition des nettoyeurs de bureau. *Les Mondes Du Travail, 7*, 75–86.

Schofield, M. (1999). "Neither master nor slave...". A practical case study in the development and employment of cleaning robots. In *1999 7th IEEE International Conference on Emerging Technologies and Factory Automation. Proceedings ETFA '99*, Barcelona (Vol. 2, pp. 1427–1434). https://doi.org/10.1109/ETFA.1999.813157

Schwartz, A., Gerberich, S. G., Albin, T., Kim, H., Ryan, A. D., Church, T. R., & Arauz, R. F. (2020). The association between janitor physical workload, mental workload, and stress: The SWEEP study. *Work, 65*(4), 837–846. https://doi.org/10.3233/WOR-203135

Simpson, R., Slutskaya, N., Lewis, P., & Höpfl, H. (2012). Introducing dirty work, concepts and identities. In R. Simpson, N. Slutskaya, P. Lewis, & H. Höpfl (Eds.), *Dirty work. Identity studies in the social sciences* (pp. 1–18). Palgrave Macmillan. https://doi.org/10.1057/9780230393530_1

Soni-Sinha, U., & Yates, C. A. B. (2013). 'Dirty work?' Gender, race and the union in industrial cleaning. *Gender, Work and Organization, 20*(6), 737–751. https://doi.org/10.1111/gwao.12006

Tapia, M., & Turner, L. (2013). Union campaigns as countermovements. *British Journal of Industrial Relations, 51*, 601–622. https://doi.org/10.1111/bjir.12035

Wills, J. (2008). Making class politics possible: Organizing contract cleaners in London. *International Journal of Urban and Regional Research, 32*(2), 305–323. https://doi.org/10.1111/j.1468-2427.2008.00783.x

Zock, J. P. (2005). World at work: Cleaners. *Occupational and Environmental Medicine, 62*(8), 581–584. https://doi.org/10.1136/oem.2004.015032

CHAPTER 5

Automation, Digitalisation, and Technological Autonomy in the Periphery. A Case Study in the Automotive Complex of Argentina

María Celeste Gómez and Carina Borrastero

Abstract In this chapter, we address the issue of technological autonomy in a peripheral industrial subsidiary through a holistic workplace-level case study at a plant within the automotive complex of Argentina. We ask whether technological change in the subsidiary is autonomous concerning the most relevant automation and digitalisation technologies introduced in the production process and which non-technological factors influence the degree of technological autonomy achieved by the plant. Over the course of a year, we conducted site tours and observations at the shop floor, semi-structured interviews with company executives, workers, union representatives, and public officials, along with the collection of quantitative and qualitative information from various secondary sources. Our main

M. C. Gómez (✉) · C. Borrastero
Centro de Investigaciones en Ciencias Económicas, Universidad Nacional de Córdoba & CONICET, Córdoba, Argentina
e-mail: mcelestegomez@unc.edu.ar

findings indicate that a hypothesis of non-technological dependence tends to prevail: the ability of the local plant to control and adapt the integration of technology into its internal organisational environment depends on intrinsic characteristics of its productive trajectory and organisational culture. These features are, in turn, strongly influenced by institutional and economic factors of the local context beyond the global technological strategies of the parent company. Although the results are specific to a single-case study, its implications might also be relevant in other settings.

Keywords Automation · Digitalisation · Automotive industry · Technological autonomy · Periphery

5.1 Introduction

The automotive industry is considered an industry of industries (ILO, 2020) due to its embedded association with the mass production and consumption paradigms of the twentieth-century economy. Its contribution to global GDP, the stimulus it provides to technological innovation within and beyond the sector, and the large investments and jobs it generates support millions of people around the world. This industry has pioneered the use of robots and cobots,[1] and 30% of all robot installations are located in the automotive industry (IFR, 2019). The adoption of digital technologies disrupts the industry's entire supply chain, from product design to vehicle sales.

In auto parts production, even higher degrees of automation and digitalisation are observed, particularly in the periphery, where automotive plants focus more on vehicle assembly (Pan, 2021).

Thus, access to technological advances—both "old" and "new" generations—is not evenly distributed along the global value chain (GVC). Despite the active participation of peripheral economies in automotive GVCs and the impact of the automotive industry on employment generation and technological capabilities in these economies (Cresti et al.,

---

[1] According to the International Federation of Robotics (IFR 2019) the term cobots refers to a typology of collaborative robots whose characteristics allow them to work in factories in coordination with people.

2023), there are few studies that address the techno-economic transformations in the automotive plants in Argentina (Civetta et al., 2023; Pan, 2021).

The objective of this work is in addressing the degree of autonomy of a local plant in undertaking technological decisions and facing the possible effects of technological dependence due to the implementation of mostly imported production models that may or may not align with local needs. This perspective is closely associated with the research line that focuses on the level of dependency/autonomy of each company regarding the adopted technology. That is, the company's ability to control and adapt the insertion of technology into its internal organisational environment (as seen in Chap. 3 of this book). We provide a series of insights on the role that the production trajectory and local institutional arrangements play in these processes of technological change in the periphery.

Therefore, our research questions read as follows:

1. Is technological change in the subsidiary firm manifested as autonomous, relatively autonomous, or heteronomous concerning the most recently introduced relevant technologies in the production processes of the plant?
2. What non-technological factors influence the degree of technological autonomy achieved by the local plant?

We adopted a qualitative methodology that allows for an in-depth exploration of a particular case and its overall context: the *holistic single-case study* developed at the workplace level (Yin, 2014). Between August 2023 and September 2024, we conducted three site tours of the entire plant and five in-depth interviews with seven key informants—executives, supervisors, workers, and union representatives—of the company. We also conducted two external interviews and developed a work session with key figures from the Provincial Government's Secretariat of Industry, specifically aimed at understanding the role of the State and local institutions in the technological investment processes of companies within the automotive complex. Finally, we examined a large variety of institutional documents, contributions from the specialised press, and empirical literature on the case.

The firm[2] is a big local subsidiary of a multinational company (MNC) located for decades in the city of Córdoba. The life cycle of the traditional products is requiring the subsidiary to undergo a productive and technological transformation by incorporating new lines of products.

We address the research questions by focusing on two specific technologies adopted in the Córdoba plant in a relatively recent period: automated guided vehicles (AGV) in the shop floor and a digital management system widely used in the company (an Enterprise Resource Planning (ERP) customised version). Starting from the analysis of these two specific technologies and their implementation, we gauge insights into the overall dynamics of automation and digitalisation technologies in the plant as a whole. Such an empirical approach will allow us to disentangle the specificities of technological change at the workplace level, its drivers, and its effects. Hence, we will be able to single out the degree of autonomy or dependency to make strategic technological and productive decisions in a peripheral subsidiary of the local automotive complex.

Although the results are specific to a single-case study, their implications might result as equally relevant in other settings.

5.2 Background and Theoretical Framework: Production, Technology and Decision in the Periphery

We assume that access to technological advances—both "old" and "new" generation—is not evenly distributed along the structure of the global value chain (GVC) of the automotive industry (Brincks et al., 2018; de Matos et al., 2019; Jürgens & Krzywdzinski, 2016; Krzywdzinski, 2017; Wenten, 2017). The relocation of MNC plants to Asian, African, and Latin American countries (with relatively lower labour costs) has not necessarily included activities related to design, research and development, and high-end product developments. Head offices in countries with high labour costs and leading knowledge endowments (e.g., Germany, Japan, France, among others) mostly carry out these activities. Instead, as the international literature identifying the existence of a smile curve at the

---

[2] In accordance with the confidentiality policy of the subsidiary, we do not identify it here or in any other section of the work, nor any characteristic of the interviewees belonging to the workforce, beyond their affiliation with the company.

world level reports (Cresti et al., 2023; Riccio et al., 2024; Stöllinger, 2021), plants in peripheral locations generally deal with the final stages in the production chain (such as assembly and tuning of vehicles) and operate with relatively lower technological standards, capturing a reduced share of the chain's value (Cresti et al., 2023; Stöllinger, 2021).

Mergers and acquisitions (M&A) have been instrumental in shaping the structure and geography of the industry, evolving along with the needs of MNCs. For decades, companies had expanded their operations into emerging markets (Rajesh Kumar, 2012). Nowadays, generalised M&A focus on functional collaboration agreements, technology, and platform sharing to find faster ways to access innovation, create new products and services, sell assets incompatible with companies' future strategies, and respond to shareholders' needs (Keienburg et al., 2019). Such operations include original equipment and component manufacturers, suppliers, and technology companies (Krzywdzinski, 2021), emphasising concentration of the production and innovation market.

In this context, the level of technological dependence/autonomy of the companies (Cirillo et al., 2023; Krzywdzinski, 2017) in the periphery is a relevant issue to consider. On the one hand, digital competencies not only derive from the characteristics and use of technology at the time of its adoption (Edwards & Ramírez, 2016). Their development also relates to previous decisions regarding their design and broader dimensions linked to organisational decisions: the choice of technology, its integration with digital and non-digital technical systems, how the capabilities are exploited or not, and how tasks and skills are redistributed among workers. On the other hand, the local institutional, political, and economic context exerts a strong influence on these processes (Gallie, 2017; Lloyd & Payne, 2023). As a result, we can find various "gradients" of adoption of new digital technologies (Ascúa, 2021) in the internal organisation of the subsidiaries, in each case resulting in some level of autonomy that allows the plant to make strategic decisions.

Thus, in this chapter we propose that decisions regarding the production strategy, the adoption of technology, and the resulting work organisation in the peripheral plant are influenced in part by internal actors within the company (Gallie, 2017; Krzywdzinski, 2017; Lloyd & Payne, 2023) and to a large extent by external factors linked to the local context, even in the case of MNC subsidiaries.

Within the automotive sector, heterogeneous corporations operate with varying degrees of autonomy regarding the technologies they implement, considering their production strategies. Some of the companies have the technological and organisational capabilities to "govern" the technologies in use; others simply adapt to technological standards within their value chains. Therefore, any evaluation of the technical change processes should consider both the role of the production profile and company governance schemes in the definition of technological strategies at the plant level and the influence of the local context on those profiles and schemes.

Considering the heterogeneity of technological patterns displayed at the firm level, several internal and external aspects play a critical role. On the intra-firm side, the technological trajectory and organisational culture, the type of innovation, and the opportunities for change (Calvino & Virgillito, 2018; Dosi & Virgillito, 2019; Montobbio et al., 2022). On the extra-firm (peripheral) side, the technological paradigms, the productive trajectory of the hub where the firm is localised, and the local institutional and economic context play a relevant role, as we will argue. The segment of the local value chain in which each company operates is also relevant, given the multiple heterogeneities related to the structural features of automotive assembly plants or auto parts manufacturers (Pan, 2021).

Studies on automation and digitalisation in the Argentinian automotive complex are scarce and mainly focus on other subject matters. Certain literature examines the technological conditions of the automotive complex and/or describes the process of digital transformation (Baruj et al., 2017; Civetta et al., 2023; Dulcich et al., 2022). Other studies focus on the reorganisation of work processes resulting from the adoption of digital technologies and the lack of capacities of labour institutions—i.e., collective bargaining—needed in order to have a direct impact on it (Nava, 2022; ILO, 2020; Pan, 2021; Raffaghelli, 2023). Finally, few studies critically review the role of the state and other institutional actors and the effectiveness of specific regulations for the automotive industry (Falvo, 2021; Garriz & Panigo, 2016). For our part, none of them addresses the technological issues regarding companies located in Córdoba, the original and currently essential hub of this industry in the country, nor have they adopted any technological dependency/autonomy approach to evaluate plant-level decisions concerning digital technologies.

5.3 Methodology

We based our study on a qualitative methodology that allows for an in-depth exploration of specific aspects of a particular case and its context: the holistic single-case study (Yin, 2014), dedicated to a single unit of analysis, a plant within the automotive complex located in Córdoba.

The selection of this company and the study of how the research problem manifests within it are based on its nature associated with that of a "revelatory case" (Yin, 2014), given the scarcity of specific background and the relevance of the topic. In this sense, following the same author, even the descriptive information obtained is revealing. Critical aspects related to the local context emerged (political and economic upswings during the research period), entailing the direction of the research questions and the working hypotheses. As Yin argues, this combination of events constitutes a strength of this type of methodology, whose challenges are overcome by applying strict protocols that we explain below.

We have developed a case study at the workplace level. For a year, we studied the Córdoba plant within its local and national context. The data collection phase involved multiple sources, both primary and secondary. After obtaining the necessary formal permissions to conduct the study as researchers from the public university, between August 2023 and May 2024 we conducted three in-person visits to explore and tour the local plant. We observed the facilities, the production processes, and the behaviour of the personnel involved. We also consulted our guides on site (a Human Resources representative, a representative from the Management Department, and a Union Delegate) about the various matters under study. For the fieldwork research, informed consent was obtained from the company, the union, the Provincial Secretariat of Industry, and individual participants to conduct interviews, record them, and publish their statements under their supervision.

During the visits or in specific additional focus meetings, we conducted five in-person interviews with six members from different areas of the company identified through a process of network (snowball) sampling: executives, supervisors, and workers from technical and administrative areas, as well as a union representative with a long-standing career in the company.

For the interviews, we used unique structured questionnaires, developed and applied according to three different profiles: technology and human resources specialists (hierarchical and non-hierarchical), and union representatives. Interviews were audio recorded and fully transcribed, except for one that could not be recorded in audio due to organisational issues within the company, but all responses to the questionnaire were recorded in writing. In each of the interviews, both authors participated, taking descriptive and analytical notes in a field notebook. In all cases, the audio recordings, transcriptions, and notes were sent to the interviewees and the company authorities responsible for the permissions, who corroborated the consistency between the content and the established agreements.

The analytical dimensions addressed include activity and other performance indicators, production and work structure, technologies adopted and local capabilities, institutional actors, and local political and economic context, as shown in Table 5.2.

Subsequent to the series of interviews at the facility level, and following the same protocols, we conducted two additional interviews with the union representative previously consulted and the Secretary of Industry of the provincial government, specifically aimed at understanding the role of the local State (the government of the province of Córdoba) in the conditions for permanence, new investments, and the productive and technological adaptation of the local plant. In Table 5.3, we detail the interviewee profiles:

In addition to the fieldwork, we analysed a large variety of institutional documents, contributions from the specialised press, and empirical literature on the case.

To validate the findings, we followed recommendations from Yin (2014). During the research design phase, as a tactic for "external validity", we derived the methodological approach and analysis dimensions from the adopted theoretical framework. In the data collection phase,

Table 5.1 Interviews conducted at the plant level

N° Int	Interview date	Length of Interview (min.)	Organisation
1	22/11/2023	90 min	Company
2	8/3/2024	97 min	Labour Union
3	22/3/2024	56 min	Company
4	27/3/2024	48 min	Company
5	22/5/2024	88 min	Company

Table 5.2 Dimensions of analysis

Dimension	Detail
Activity	Structural data and basic performance indicators of the firm
Production	Products and processes currently developed
Technology	Core technologies and production models
	Recently adopted 4.0 or digital technologies
	Projects for the short- and medium-term effective integration of digital technologies
	IT Management and technological integration: dynamics of technologically managed problem resolution, capabilities, and limitations (beyond and within subsidiary, actors involved)
	The technological prospects: the impact of the macroeconomic and political context on the course of the decision and technological investment at the sector and the plant level
	The effects of technology integration on jobs and tasks at the level of industrial process
Work	Trade Union role: perspective on technological change and labour relations
	Workers' receptivity and engagement at various stages of the adoption of technologies
GVC	Location of the subsidiary in the GVC of the company
	Technological capabilities of the subsidiary
	Decision-making capacity of the subsidiary on technological adoption and development
Context	Influence of local political and economic context on the definition of the subsidiaries productive and technological strategy

Table 5.3 Interviews on state role dimensions

N° Int	Interview date	Length of interview (min.)	Sector of activity	Gender	Seniority (years)
6	18/9/2024	31 min	Labour Union	M	16
7	24/9/2024	29 min	Provincial Government—Secretary of Industry	M	1

to ensure "constructive validity", we used multiple sources of evidence, established an evidence chain between the interviewees profiting from the snowballing approach, and subjected the interview results to review by key informants. Finally, to ensure "reliability", we implemented unified question guides for similar interviewee profiles. During the interviews, as expected, we found a link between the responses and the general perceptions of the executives, as well as the emergence of specific dimensions regarding challenges to overcome or to be addressed, particularly among the workers and the union representative.

5.4 Results and Main Findings

5.4.1 The Company, the Productive Process and the Local Landscape of Automotive Production

Argentina is one of the 49 countries in the world with a long-standing automotive industry, currently occupying the 24th place as a world producer (MECON, 2023). The complex represents nearly 1% of the GDP and 4.5% of the industrial value added (INDEC, 2023). It also absorbs 0.6% and 3.4% of the total and industrial registered employment, respectively (OEDE, 2024). In terms of exports, this industry is the second most important complex in the country, with 13.3% of the export value (INDEC, 2023).

The city of Córdoba, located in the central area and demographically and economically the second largest in the country with 1.5 million inhabitants, has historically been a preferred destination for the automotive MNCs for its potential and accumulated techno-industrial capabilities, and its specially qualified human resources (both in the industry and the large number of educational institutions at different levels). Local plants from companies such as Fiat, Iveco, and Renault-Nissan together employ more than 5,000 people in the sector (Giannoni, 2022) and cooperate with more than 250 auto parts companies.

The local plant, which reports to its headquarters outside Latin America and a regional corporate head, has been producing and exporting from Córdoba to various countries around the world for several decades. Currently, it manufactures different types of products, involving two coexisting production models: one type involves a high degree of automation (conveyor lines, robots, and AGVs), while the other resembles assembly activities based primarily on human labour.

Work is organised in a cellular format and by technological families. It is possible for workers to scale up in the matrix by acquiring new knowledge, and scaling up impacts wages. This cellular system enhances the effectiveness of continuous improvement systems and monitoring, as it coordinates reports from workers themselves and their supervisors. In addition, there are options of in-person technical training careers, implemented in the plant, that workers can optionally enrol in.

It can be said that there is also a culture of independent and autonomous training, which is expressed, for example, in the case of the maintenance of AGVs, which are operated by outsourced personnel but intervened by a permanent staff worker of the company with programming skills who devotes their working hours to operating and repairing these devices, even without being formally assigned to this task.

In terms of management of digital technologies, an ERP system is implemented. Some of the functions are related to the basic human resources (HR) tasks (attendance and punctuality control, life events, salary settlement, among others), the description of the routines and procedures that the specialised human resource performs, and, also the internal communications automatically orientated to specific workers according to the purpose of the communication. At the time of writing, the plant is gradually migrating from its traditional ERP module to a newer, interactive, and more comprehensive one.

The productive and technological changes are currently unfolding at a critical time for local industry. Over an extended period of 14 years, the value added of the automotive industry declined by 28.1%, while the number of registered jobs fell by 5.6%. In recent months, Argentina's dire situation has become worse. After a new government took office at the end of 2023, it implemented a series of radical neoliberal policies that worsened the crisis. Particularly, the value added of the automotive industry fell by 18.5% annually in the first quarter of 2024; this trend persisted in the following months and has affected the manufacturing sector (INDEC, 2024).

However, given the importance of this production complex for the city and the province, there is a local culture of protecting automotive employment, which involves the firm itself.

5.4.2 Overview of the Main Findings

We put forward two guiding questions on the issue of technological autonomy/dependence in a peripheral industrial subsidiary.

Initially, we asked whether technological change in the subsidiary is autonomous, relatively autonomous, or heteronomous concerning the most recently introduced digital technologies in the plant's production processes. The first finding that emerged from the case is that there is no clear-cut answer to this question. There are two closely associated orders of technological autonomy/dependence in this peripheral subsidiary that go beyond the link with the technologies themselves:

Relationship with the technical systems and their suppliers. We observe that the plant is not dependent on AGVs and automation technologies in general at its current stage, although it is dependent on the ERP system as a newly introduced digitalisation technology. Therefore, regarding automation technologies, production processes can unfold without the systems imposing strong constraints, even in the face of structural problems in implementation or failures in the provision of services by suppliers. As for digitalisation technologies, we observed strong restrictions to the autonomous development of the subsidiary associated with the configuration of the systems themselves and the type of links that this implies with the headquarters and the suppliers.

Autonomy/heteronomy of the peripheral subsidiary in the technological decision chain with respect to the different technical systems. On the one hand, the subsidiary is relatively autonomous from the parent company and the regional corporate head in deciding to adopt new automation technologies at the shop floor and to use existing ones by adapting them to contextual changes (demand and supply constraints). On the other hand, it is not autonomous regarding digitalisation technologies, where the pace of adoption is much more frequent, it is defined at the regional level, and adaptation to the external context is not a relevant parameter.

Secondly, we asked what other non-technological factors that can be captured through the perspective of actors within the establishment influence the degree of technological autonomy achieved in the local plant. Among the main dimensions, we found: local organisational culture; corporate productive decisions within the framework of the impending end of the life cycle of one of the products traditionally manufactured at the plant; economic and institutional hurdles and opportunities imposed by the local context.

In sum, the nature of the technologies implemented, the way in which the technological decision process unfolds, and the relationship with local actors involved in the development of its activity affect the power of the local plant vis-à-vis the parent to operate on its own. The way this local power is exercised mostly depends on non-technological drivers: the degree of technological decision-making autonomy achieved by the peripheral subsidiary within the framework of the corporate structure and the influence of local contextual factors.

5.4.3 Technologies and Autonomy/Dependence Relationships of the Local Subsidiary

At the plant, the adoption of new production technologies is carried out under the business case methodology, which consists of a technical, organisational and financial evaluation of their incorporation. This might originate from an internal proposal from the engineering areas to improve a process or from an external opportunity (i.e., a sale or transfer offer from another plant or from a supplier). In the case of robots, they were acquired following the implementation of a new production line to perform tasks such as twinning of parts/assemblies, turning and oiling of parts, fulfilling ergonomic functions, and reducing personnel costs in repetitive activities of simple processes that do not require supervision. AGVs, incorporated at the suggestion of the local plant, replaced functions previously performed by personnel from an outsourced logistics company, and their introduction has not resulted in the replacement of workers.

For both robots and AGVs, the suppliers are external and foreign, and the acquisition was financed with external funds provided by the company's regional division. Such suppliers have a significant initial involvement in the implementation process by training users and then progressively withdraw from the process to act as the support of last resort.

Robots require initial programming and maintenance and do not require ongoing customisation. Regarding these technologies, there were no major implementation problems (Int. 1). But regarding the AGVs, the implementation process was different: some of the trolleys are not operative currently due to technical problems (Int. 1), but the plant continues to operate smoothly, with no automatic transfer of parts from the outside warehouses to the workstations, no replacement of workers, managers, or supervisors, and no downgrading of their hierarchies (Int. 1; Int. 2; Int. 3).

The adoption of these technologies has also not led to an overload on the manual or intellectual tasks of the staff, although they do require permanent programming of low complexity. Both the evaluation of the company's members and that of the union representative agree on this point:

> What the colleague has to do... let's see: how might things have changed for him? He must be more attentive; there will be a robot that will come to look for a pile of boxes, and the robot doesn't know if the pieces are correctly or incorrectly placed. However, he also has to have everything in order: these pieces have to be organised in the same way, right? The times are production times. You know that you have to make 400 pieces a day, and you have to leave them in one place. I can assure you that just because the vehicle is there, they are not going to make more [products].
>
> Int. 2, Union Representative.

From technical and administrative areas are also constantly highlighting the learning process involved in adopting this technology at the plant (Int. 1; Int. 2).

The introduction of new technologies has required new workers' skills, such as programming and maintenance of devices. Specialised training for programmers and electronic engineers is developed on the job, under the strategy of maintaining human resources endowment and keeping working as much as possible with in-house staff (Int. 1).

In the case of the more advanced ERP, the process of adoption and implementation (in progress at the time of writing this chapter) is developing differently. The decision-making process is top-down, given the company structure, just as the suppliers are foreign in all its layers (Int. 3, 5).

Furthermore, the very characteristics of the technology impose restrictions on the autonomy of the Córdoba plant and its staff to intervene in the technical system in order to modify or adapt it to local needs:

> We have something that is very strong, which is software security. There are certain systems that enable cybersecurity that establish, "there is something to write text." The authorised tool is [name under confidentiality]. It's connected. Or, for example, we have to use [web browsers under confidentiality]. OK? Those are the official ones. The others are blocked, or you can't log in. They're the ones that don't have viruses. In other words, the system is quite structural with that.
> What happens is that [the ERP] is a square, I mean, you can't get out of it. It's like Linux and Windows: you touched one thing too many, you put

a little dot on it, it exploded, and it's not good anymore. Well, [the ERP] is Windows; I mean, if it doesn't work, it gives you a giant error message. It doesn't allow you.

Int. 5, Company Informant.

Finally, we note that the delocalisation of the implementation decision and management process, coupled with the limited funding provided by the corporate headquarters, prevented access to the most advanced version of the technological tool. This imposes additional restrictions on system integration, a sort of technological lock-in that makes the company dependent on a specific system and its supplier, making it difficult or costly to switch to alternative solutions:

> A technological change is taking place that means that the [ERP] organisation, which is an international system, is managed by "X" from [another country], and X is sent a paper saying that from now on he has to pay a 4% increase. He doesn't remember that he has to charge it on all the items that we charge, so from there comes "Hey, you have to modify...".
> I'm going to tell you something else that is a problem. Do you know Canva? The design tool? Well, if you don't have the Pro and you want to put more beautiful music, you can't do it because you have to pay.

Int. 2, Union Representative.

Nevertheless, it is important to note that, in the view of the HR personnel consulted (hierarchical and not hierarchical), there is a positive general impact of the ERP on the work process and the workers (freeing up time) because of the incorporation of the new system.

5.4.4 Technological Skills Accumulation and Shop Floor Culture

Concerning factors not linked to specific technologies and their impact on the degree of autonomy/heteronomy of the subsidiary in the process of technological adoption, several important features of the local firm should be highlighted. These are associated with the local organisational culture, the general level of accumulated technological competences, and specific demands of workers' protection. These local conditions and constraints have historically promoted the corporate decision to maintain the plant in its current localisation, together with the strategy of opening new business units in times of crisis or technological paradigm shifts and the regulatory and political-economic difficulties that the local context imposes on the activity of these kinds of factories in Argentina.

An Organisational Culture That Enables the Emergence of Voices and Actions of Contribution and Resistance to Technological Change That, at the End of the Day, Ends up Benefiting Local Workers

A relevant issue that emerges from the interviews and observations conducted (including the union representative's view) is the space that plant workers have to express their needs related to their daily productive activities, contribute ideas regarding the organisation of production at the micro level, and, occasionally, block certain changes planned by management through concrete acts of resistance on the shop floor. The inclusion of these voices is not necessarily channelled through formal spaces or initiatives but is part of the organisational culture ingrained over the decades.

> If the operator wants to use a machine that is not intended to be used, you're going to say no, but you're going to go to the plant floor, and you're going to see that he's using it. And if he doesn't want to use a new machine, he's not going to do it, no matter what you tell him. Maybe we are too sensitive to the workers' opinion. We all know each other; we are like a family. The biggest resistance that can sometimes appear is not "why that machine" but "¿why didn't you tell me you were going to put it in?"
>
> Int. 1, Company Informant.

That "like a family" context was palpable for the researchers during the various visits to the workplace: in a complex of thousands of people and more than 5 separate buildings, most of them know each other by name, greet each other enthusiastically, and seem to have some time for social interaction beyond the strictly work-related one.

Meanwhile, the trade union as a local actor maintains an important role in the dynamics of organisational change resulting from technological change.

> When they must implement some system, they call, and they hold meetings by cell, by sector, and they tell them. There is usually a delegate at that meeting. Then they say: "We talked to the union." The delegate says, "Yes, they talked to the union." Well, we come out of that meeting with the

company, we get together with the delegates, and we say, "The company offered this; we asked for this." If we agree, the company is going to come down and "sell" this [name under confidentiality] system. If nobody says so, it's because there was no agreement. But since the company needs it, it also agrees to the union's request.

Int. 2, Union Representative.

Moreover, the workers themselves engage in forms of micro-resistance that are often specifically related to the rigidity of certain technical systems in relation to the daily work dynamics they are accustomed to. These informal modes of micro-resistance at times have some impact on the technology adoption curve within the company, although they do not hinder the effective implementation of the most relevant technological strategies.

> The introduction of new technologies is not discussed. The benefits are discussed. In reality, [the system name under confidentiality] is an introduction of a new working methodology. You know how long it lasted, don't you? It lasted three months. Why? Because afterwards they often become unfeasible, these very strong systems.

Int. 2, Union Representative.

Although it is worth noting that, from the union's point of view, the autonomy of the local plant in making productive and technological decisions is less than what the second- and third-line executives and referents interviewed tend to highlight. Nevertheless, the local actors have both the opportunities and the capacity to take advantage of this room for manoeuvring to generate benefits for the workers that the company promotes too:

> The concept comes down to a question of "with me or without me." That's the concept, ok? If the factory has this thing that came from [headquarters], what are they going to do? They are going to do it. You will be able to say no, you will deny it, and you will fight it, but they are going to do it anyway, in a different way, with a different name; we already know that. So, what is the objective of not saying no: "I'm not saying no, go ahead, implement it, but in exchange we want this", and that's how a lot of things were achieved, improvements in the system of categories, for example.

Int. 2, Union Representative.

At the same time, these opportunities to take advantage of technological changes, so deeply rooted in the organisational culture, are closely linked to the non-substitutive nature of the technologies implemented and thus, the relevance that labour continues to hold in the production processes of the peripheral plant:

> The company told us, "We are going to set up a plant, where we are going to set up [product name under confidentiality], and we are going to incorporate [number under confidentiality] workers." "Great." What we... maybe because there were no people left outside, I don't know why, and we realised this later, that productivity was going to be so high.

Int. 2, Union Representative.

A High Level of Technological Skills for the Deployment of the Plant's Activity, Despite the Cyclically Difficult Local Context

> I think it is important to mention that [the most recent productive facility] has a very advanced level of technology. In other words, if you go to any plant in [headquarters], there are the same machines and the same level of technology. Because there is that prejudice that "Ah, well, surely in Argentina, they make it easier or of lower quality, or the machines are more crude." The same machines that are used in, and I say, first-world countries like [name under confidentiality], the same level of technology, and the same brand are the ones we use here. We have complications, as do all companies [because of] the current situation in the country. It is often difficult to bring a machine and to bring the corresponding spare parts. Surely in [headquarters country] a machine breaks down and the machine supplier is next door; you just have to take it off the shelf and give it to him.

Int. 4, Company Informant.

A remarkable finding from the study is that, despite being located in the periphery and within the difficult Argentine economic context, the technological capabilities of the local plant are not only significant but also recognised by the headquarters themselves:

> In general, in the Cordoba plant, if you look at this far, you will see all the [awards won under confidentiality]. In terms of quality, we are very proud. In terms of technology, there are processes and many things that were developed because one person came up with them or because they liked them. Locally. And they [the local leaders] gave space to that initiative. Well, [the internal training programme] was a great achievement. From [headquarters] they were asking us how we managed. I didn't think that it would have such an impact and that something that we do would be so good, right? In other words, something new and novel, but within what would be normal for us. Well, the [trained internally] guys themselves are really cool. They're developing a robot, a mechanical arm, and a [robot: name under confidentiality]. They're putting it back together from scratch; it's broken, and it's lying around. All the technicians from [the headquarters] came—the electricians, the mechanics, the electronics, everything. No, "I couldn't.". One of the maintenance guys came, erased the whole system, and did it all from scratch. That system was then being asked for. In other words, they asked us again, from the company that makes that machine.
>
> Int. 5, Company Informant.

The organisational culture and accumulated technological competences lead to the roots of a technological learning vocation. Very diverse technological decisions are evaluated and made according to local conditions and needs, which applies both to digitalisation and automation technologies. The self-taught nature of many of these learning processes is another associated feature that stands out.

> We have people who are fans of programming and those kinds of issues, who have been getting closer. This is the case of "X", say, the AGV subject. He follows it very closely, but on his own initiative, it is not even of the area, not even a task of his, but he does it by his own will. Here, by the type of structure we have, we should conduct that through [formal technical areas], which are the ones that investigate and optimise the processes or study new alternative tools. There are always technologies that one is looking at and is trying to reach. It's always about running the line of knowledge a degree further. Always.
>
> Int. 4, Company Informant.

> Like those in the electronics lab. They've... broke a plate, and already the replacement has taken two or three days or this "And, no, but we can see

here, because we welded this, I have one stored in a drawer", and it has a box full of electronic components, and they change and test. That you didn't know it existed.

Int. 4, Company Informant.

These kinds of local micro-innovation dynamics include not only the type of execution activities mentioned in the quotations but also intellectual contributions from workers to executives, which "many even take as a personal challenge" (Int. 4).

The local firm also operates a system of formal and informal recognition that contributes to strengthening these dynamics, which is very consolidated in the company's working culture:

> Everyone knows the role they play, and you know that if you are interested in something and you strive, you will be able to develop it and they will give you a place, and if you don't, you'll stay where you are, but it's all right. Always in the absence of dismissal as the policy of the firm. The more you know, the more you earn.

Int. 4, Company Informant.

Also, recognised workers are invited to business trips, receive informal up-down social invitations on the hierarchical line, or enjoy informal terms of employment with differential benefits (for example, defining their working hours and rotating between positions) (Int. 1).

The history and roots of the plant in the local environment, along with the age and effective trajectory of many employees who started in positions of relatively low skills and ascended to higher hierarchies over time, also play a role (Int. 3, Int. 5).

5.4.5 *Productive Reconversion, Local Context and Technological Change*

Within the framework of the general evolution of the productive paradigm of the automotive industry, the plant is undergoing a significant productive reconversion process, which requires the implementation of new technologies and production methodologies, a task that is often quite challenging in Argentina. We argue that the decision to maintain local production despite the difficulties and costs of techno-productive transformation, exacerbated by the challenges of the Argentinian economic and regulatory context and the recurrent crises in the country, is significantly related to local factors that drive the materialisation of the company's productive and technological projects at the existing plant versus its relocation.

On the one hand, the importance of the Córdoba plant for the company itself is a main finding of the study. The accumulated productive and technological capacities we have mentioned are a value for the company (Int. 5, 6).

At the same time, different levels of the government architecture have a direct engagement with the long-term policies and the productive transformation of these kinds of companies, given their economic weight in the local industrial and labour structure.

Before analysing the specific local factors of Córdoba, it is worthwhile to highlight the significance that key informants attribute to the national regulatory and economic context in the techno-productive strategies. In this sense, corporations may or may not adopt these strategies once they have been operating in the country for some time (both during industrial crises and recovery periods). From our point of view, both levels of influence—national and local—are part of the specific drivers of the company's productive and technological strategies.

In the words of the trade union representative, the general influence of the national political-economic context for the automotive industry, and the local conditions is very strong:

> Development of the local industry resulted in passing from 3,500 to 10,000 [workers]. At the national level, from circa 40 thousand, it reached 114,000. It is not that we were looking for people on the street; it is that new opportunities began to open, and the sector grew enormously. The political decision to make the country a productive, industrial country, to develop an industry that is not just a raw material. To that they added the "flex" [trade policy instrument] with Brazil, because we brought a lot of models from Brazil. When you set up a bilateral negotiation with Brazil and you say, "Look, you can get in for a dollar, and I can send you a dollar" [the flex]. So, here you could see a lot of Brazilian cars, but what no one could see is that in Argentina they sold about 1 million cars, and they produced about one million cars, because they were sold to Mexico and Brazil, which was, say, the boom of the year 2014.

Int. 2, Union Representative.

The comment refers to the previous cycle of economic and industrial policy, when a developmentalist political group was in power. Currently, the shift from the orientation that governments had since 2003 to the triumph of the present "libertarian" far-right government has resulted in a deep economic and political crisis that directly affects the manufacturing activity levels.[3,4] Nevertheless, even in this context, MNCs like the company under study find opportunities to improve their investment, production, and technology outlooks, which, in turn, positively impact employment and its sustainability at the local level during times of crisis. In this case, regulatory changes aimed at trade liberalisation, driven by the new government, would enable the company to negotiate alliances with other firms to develop new lines of products at the local plant as part of its productive transformation (Int. 6).

For its part, Argentina's labour institutional framework and the historical strength of industrial unions, particularly in the automotive sector, provide additional determinants for the conditions necessary for companies to remain in the territory. Although in Argentina in the twenty-first century collective bargaining agreements became moderately centralised (at the branch level), some cases—such as that of our firm—maintain negotiations at the company level. Both the original agreement signed with the national government and its updates have a high degree of specificity, which reinforces the strong propensity for employment protection in the local sector and the subsidiary at the regulatory level. It includes the definition of daily and monthly paid staff and the categorisation of workers in areas. The agreements combine this taxonomy with criteria for educational skills, experience, and tasks, including an occupational evaluation system. Yet, vernacular negotiation culture operates strongly, beyond the legal frameworks, on the results that are actually achieved in this regard.

---

[3] For the manufacturing sector, the accumulated level of activity in the first seven months of 2024 was 12.5% shorter than its equivalent of 2023, and 6.3% lower than the same period the year before for the auto parts segment. Yet, the employment data (with certain lagging) shows that the total manufacturing jobs for the first quarter in 2024 is 0.1% lower than the equivalent for 2023, and 0.9% lower for the auto parts segment.

[4] In fact, the crisis in the sector affected the development of the fieldwork in terms of the difficulty in carrying out the interviews and the visits to the plants.

Regarding preventive crisis processes, in the case of [the company], it was implemented at some point. Most of the time when the company faced a crisis, we sought not to enter a preventive crisis process because that doesn't benefit the company as a whole. Whatever the agreement stipulates, with an end date but without a set programme.

Int. 6, Union Representative.

Regarding the local actors and institutionalists, the provincial state of Córdoba has a key role in creating concrete conditions for the permanence of large companies in the territory, with the techno-productive transformation that this may imply. During the completion of this work, the Governor met with the company executives more than once to discuss possible solutions to the current crisis of the Córdoba plant. The Minister of Production and the Secretary of Industry of the Province (whom we interviewed) also did so, being closely familiar with the case. Additionally, the province adhered to the national incentive regime for large investments (RIGI),[5] involving the local industrial federation.

It is also important not to lose sight of the investment cycles inherent to the corporate sector within which the strategies for each factory at the global level are integrated. Nevertheless, investments are realised in specific territories according to the national and local conditions that incentivise or hinder the permanence and productive transformation of companies' locations in the territory.

The investment cycle is coming, and it's a clear indicator that countries where the plants are located are logically chosen, point one. And secondly, subnational governments where the plants are located. For example, we have assembly plants in Córdoba, Santa Fe, and Buenos Aires. Well, the one in Santa Fe, which is also in an investment cycle, has packed up and is leaving. Córdoba has maintained its position so far. Buenos Aires has also maintained its investment cycles. Toyota has confirmed investments. Peugeot and Stellantis have confirmed investments. But let's put this in context: we are receiving less than 10% of the total investments announced for the region. For all investment data regarding assembly plants in South America, Argentina accounts for less than 10%. This positively impacts

---

[5] See https://www.cba24n.com.ar/cordoba/llaryora-anuncio-ante-el-g6-y-el-agro-que-cordoba-adherira-alrigi_a66b3ff0be362d40211464d38, https://www4.hcdn.gob.ar/dependencias/dsecretaria/Periodo2024/PDF2024/TP2024/0018-D-2024.pdf.

Córdoba because it's a significant number, right? But this is a signal: whether due to scale or more stable macroeconomic conditions or production incentive policies, investments are being decided in other markets, not in Argentina. Brazil.

Int. 7, Secretary of Industry from the Government of the Province of Córdoba.

In response to these challenges, the provincial government aims to establish an institutional framework that facilitates fluid connections with large firms.[6] In this context, two articulated policies were developed to promote major investments in Córdoba since the beginning of the twenty-first century.

The first one is a tradition of agreements with large-scale industries (especially automotive) for the establishment of plants and the creation and protection of (direct and indirect) jobs. These treaties with MNCs are then legally endorsed to provide greater institutionalisation.

> There is a very strong focus on trying to provide as many tools or incentives to companies as possible so that the decision to "pack up and leave" does not occur. Knowing that we are in a context of the country's macroeconomics that has laws allowing for continuity, but these laws, or the macro perspective, can also have twists and turns that can throw you off course. The worst thing that can happen to the subnational government is for a company to suddenly pack up because then we have 1,000, 1,200, or 1,500 direct jobs lost, plus the additional impacts, right? It is much easier to make the effort to keep them than to have to make the effort to contain the fallout, no matter how you look at it.

Int. 7, Secretary of Industry from the Government of the Province of Córdoba.

The second is the creation of organisations that articulate public–private activity. The executive bodies of these institutions comprise private, government, and academic representatives.

---

[6] The correspondence between the government discourse regarding this policy and its real impacts on the local productive fabric can be confronted with other studies that address the local industrial development policies, obtaining the same results (Borrastero & Castellani, 2018).

What does Córdoba do in terms of industrial policy? It has two attributes that differentiate it from other subnational economies. First, there is stability in that industrial policy or productive policy remains consistent. The aim is to change conditions as little as possible to allow it to happen. The second point is that there is a significant public–private collaboration. This is not only in the back-and-forth regarding the needs and the policies that respond to those needs, but also a large part of the institutions, agencies, or bodies that carry out part of the productive policy have private sector representatives in their governance structures holding the highest positions.

So, it's not just rhetorical, nor does it occur merely in the back-and-forth of conversation; the private sector also participates in the governance of institutions that implement part of the industrial policy. Examples include the Pro Córdoba Agency,[7] the Competitiveness Agency,[8] and the Innovate and Entrepreneurship Agency,[9] all chaired by members of the private sector. Additionally, the board of directors is equally divided between representatives of the state and the private sector and, in the case of the Competitiveness Agency, also includes representatives from academia.

Int. 7, Secretary of Industry from the Government of the Province of Córdoba.

This strategy allows for prior coordination before the public announcements of investments and even makes specific legal arrangements less relevant. The coordination is close, and the historical local negotiation culture—once again—prevails over the law (which does not prohibit multinational corporations from leaving the territory) and over the crises. In a sense, an MNC based in the province cannot simply relocate exclusively according to corporate strategies and needs.

The institutions that represent the sector, whether it's the Metalworking Industrialists' Chamber, the Industrial Union of Córdoba, or the Córdoba Chamber of Foreign Trade, play a very important role here because it is through them that [the companies] occupy positions in the various governance bodies I mentioned earlier. While there are laws that establish the Agencies and regulations outlining how representation works in

---

[7] See https://www.procordoba.org/quienes-somos-6902.html.
[8] See https://innovaryemprendercba.com.ar/la-agencia/.
[9] See https://competitividadcba.org/.

their governance structures, there is no specific law detailing how these connections are made. Instead, these connections occur naturally through other laws and dynamics.

Int. 7, Secretary of Industry from the Government of the Province of Córdoba.

In our case, the local context and the orientation of institutional arrangements are a necessary condition for the firm, given the significance of the integration of the local components into the company's global supply chain:

> The fluctuations of a national economy on the decisions made by the parent companies undoubtedly have an impact, but just as they have an impact, there are times when you have "to let some water pass under the bridge" because it is much more costly to stop producing something that is consumed worldwide than to rely on a small market. And with the level of integration it [the local plant] has, the impact it has on a global scale allows it to withstand some abrupt changes, particularly those driven by macroeconomic factors.

Int. 7, Secretary of Industry from the Government of the Province of Córdoba.

In this framework, fieldwork shows once again that the dynamics of technological adoption in the plant are more subject to decisions on productive reconversion and the demands of the local context than to a technological strategy or to the nature of certain technologies themselves.

From the point of view of the company, the introduction of new lines of products involves technological changes, but not necessarily towards greater automation or digitalisation, but rather those changes that better fit the new chosen production to keep their local facilities operational (for example, towards more manual tasks).

From the trade union's point of view (Int. 2), the permanence of the plant in Córdoba and the technological dynamics that it entails are associated with the general need to maintain employment in the local automotive industry for the firm itself, and the productive and technological strategies at the level of the plant must adapt to this purpose within the framework of the currently existing productive conditions.

Finally, the impact of the local economic and regulatory context—national or provincial—on the possibilities of introducing new technologies varies depending on whether they are automation or digitalisation technologies, whose "governance"—as we have already explained—is relatively differentiated.

With reference to the implementation of the new version of the ERP, a regional and delocalised strategy, a company referent interviewed said:

> Sometimes it doesn't influence so much because it's software; it's a service. If it were something material, some hardware, in that sense it would indeed involve more difficulty about customs revenue and all those things. It was planned before, but a crisis that comes suddenly does nothing to you. It may come up, it may, but I don't think there's a problem. [In software] there are some spending restrictions around there, say. To say, "Let's not spend," or "There is no money," say. So, we postpone it, we pass it forward, but that's all.

Int. 5, Company Informant.

But informants from technical areas point out that the main difficulties presented in the plant when incorporating new technologies at the shop floor are linked on the local restrictions to that investment decision, derived from the macroeconomic and political instability of Argentina, so that contextual factors weigh more heavily than technological ones right from the adoption evaluation phase (Int. 1).

5.5 Final Remarks

To conduct this study on automation, digitalisation, and technological autonomy in the periphery, we posed two initial research questions: one aimed at elucidating the degree of autonomy of the analysed subsidiary from the most recently incorporated digital technologies, and the other aimed at identifying non-technological factors that strongly influence the processes of technology adoption. Throughout the chapter, we have seen that both sets of issues, in the case of a peripheral subsidiary, are closely related to each other: the local plant's ability to control and adapt the insertion of technology into its internal organisational environment (the non-technological dependence hypothesis) relies on intrinsic characteristics of its productive trajectory and organisational culture that are, in turn, strongly influenced by institutional and economic factors of the local context beyond the global technological strategies of the parent.

We began by observing the dynamics of adoption and implementation of two digital technologies of different natures: a non-critical automation technology at the shop floor level (AGV) and a technology for the digitalisation of critical administrative processes adopted by the company at the regional level (ERP). However, addressing these units of analysis was not enough to understand the determinants and implications of technological change in the local plant, so the study was expanded to include productive and technological processes in general. In analysing this set of processes, we were able to observe how the technological strategy of a local subsidiary can be more autonomous at the level of production-related technologies (AGV) than at the level of management technologies (ERP), given the nature and number of specific challenges that need to be overcome in factory production processes, the limited degree of integration that certain state-of-the-art technologies still have in this industry on the periphery, and different institutional and context factors.

Three pillars of the local plant organisation grant it an active role in the decision-making regarding investment, production, and technological change of the parent company, which result in a non-negligible level of technological autonomy despite its subordinate position in the firm's production chain:

- A local organisational culture that enables the emergence of voices and actions of contribution and resistance.
- A high level of technological skills, which are largely generated internally, despite the cyclical difficulties that the context imposes on the productive and technological transformation of industrial plants.
- A significant role of local institutional settings in the technological investment decisions of the MNC from the industrial sector that has historically shaped the productive trajectory of the local automotive complex.

The manifestation and spaces of autonomy/heteronomy that matter most, are related to the subsidiary's position of the plant in the firm's value chain when it comes to decisions about adoption, usage, adaptation and evolution of the technologies that have already been introduced. This is not to say that there are no technical or corporate governance constraints. Rather, these constraints acquire a particular significance based on how the technological decision is organised within the corporation and how the final configuration of the new technologies is related to other factors. The national context, the territorial enclave with the history of the sector and its roots in the local culture, along with corporate, state, and union strategies of overcoming crises under the decision to maintain local production, play decisive roles in the productive trajectory and technological adoption in the local subsidiary. Against all technological determinism, technological autonomy/dependence in a peripheral subsidiary is mediated by institutional and contextual factors specific to its organisational nature and institutional settings specific to the local level. Such factors should not be disregarded when analysing the dynamics of technological adoption and its determinants within multinational companies.

Acknowledgments We are deeply grateful to the plant's management and employees for embracing us, giving of their time, and sharing their personal narratives. To the union representative who gave us our first connections and helped us with our work every step of the way. To protect the confidentiality agreement made with the corporation about its identity, we have not named either of the two organisations here. To the Secretary of Industry of the Province of Córdoba, who warmly welcomed us into his office for an extensive interview, and to the employees of that department who gave vital information for our research over several weeks. Additionally, we would like to express our gratitude to Maria Enrica Virgillito and her other editors for their contributions to academic collaboration between the North and South, as well as for their consistently perceptive remarks. Finally, we must emphasise how crucial it is for Argentina to have a top-notch public scientific and technological framework in order to do this kind of research.

References

Ascúa, R. (2021). Industry 4.0 in manufacturing SMEs of Argentina and Brazil. *Journal of the International Council for Small Business*, 2(3), 203–222. https://doi.org/10.1080/26437015.2021.1899773.

Baruj, G, Obaya, M., Porta, F., Santarcangelo, J., Sessa, C., & Zweig, I. (2017). El complejo automotriz argentino: situación tecnológica, restricciones y oportunidad. *Centro Interdisciplinario de Estudios en ciencia, Tecnología e Innovación*. Informe Técnico No. 8. http://hdl.handle.net/11336/110818

Borrastero, C., & Castellani, A. (2018). Estado y empresarios en la configuración de ámbitos estratégicos de acumulación: El caso del sector Software Córdoba, Argentina (2000–2013). *Revista Estado y Políticas Públicas, 10*, 171–193. Retrieved December 02, 2024, from https://revistaeypp.flacso.org.ar/files/revistas/1539816913_171-193.pdf

Brincks, C., Domański, B., Klier, T., & Rubenstein, J. M. (2018). Integrated peripheral markets in the auto industries of Europe and North America. *International Journal of Automotive Technology and Management, 18*(1), 1–28. https://doi.org/10.1504/IJATM.2/018.090170

Calvino, F., & Virgillito, M. E. (2018). The innovation-employment nexus: A critical survey of theory and empirics. *Journal of Economic Surveys, 32*(1), 83–117. https://doi.org/10.1111/joes.12190

Cirillo, V., Massimo, M. Rinaldini, J. Staccioli, & Virgillito M. E. (2023). Monopoly power upon the world of work: a workplace analysis in the logistic segment under automation. *LEM Working Papers Series,* 2023/44. Retrieved December 02, 2024, from https://www.lem.sssup.it/WPLem/files/2023-44.pdf

Civetta, A., Mauro, L., & Manzo, F. (2023). Transitando el camino de la transformación digital: lecciones de la industria automotriz argentina. *Revista de Economía Política de Buenos Aires, 27*, 105–142. Retrieved December 02, 2024, from http://bibliotecadigital.econ.uba.ar/download/ecopoli/ecopoli_v17_n27_04.pdf

Cresti, L., Dosi, G., Riccio, F., & Virgillito, M. E. (2023). Italy and the trap of GVC downgrading: Labour dependence in the European geography of production. *Italian Economic Journal, 9*(3), 869–906. https://doi.org/10.1007/s40797-023-00251-5

de Matos, H. H., Dias A., & Bagno R. (2019). Incremental and 'radical' innovation in an emergent country automotive subsidiary: Is there any organisational ambidexterity there? *International Journal of Automotive Technology and Management, 19*(3–4), 206–228. Retrieved December 02, 2024, from https://www.inderscienceonline.com/doi/abs/10.1504/IJATM.2019.100911

Dosi, G., & Virgillito, M. E. (2019). Whither the evolution of the contemporary social fabric? New technologies and old socioeconomic trends. *International Labour Review, 158*(4), 593–625. https://doi.org/10.1111/ilr.12145

Dulcich, F., Porta, F., Ubogui, M., & Baruj, G. (2022). The transition to electric mobility: Opportunities for the automotive value chain in Argentina. *International Journal of Automotive Technology and Management, 22*(3), 374–400. https://doi.org/10.1504/IJATM.2022.124829

Edwards, P., & Ramirez, P. (2016). When should workers embrace or resist new technology? *New Technology, Work and Employment, 31*(2), 99–113. https://doi.org/10.1111/ntwe.12067

Falvo, M. (2021). The structuring of state political opportunities towards and from capital and labor in the case of the automotive industry in Argentina (2000–2015). *Studia Politica. Romanian Political Science Review, 21*(1), 121–149. Retrieved December 02, 2024, from https://www.ceeol.com/search/article-detail?id=968685

Gallie, D. (2017). The quality of work in a changing labour market. *Social Policy and Administration, 51*(2), 226–243. https://doi.org/10.1111/spol.12285

Gárriz, A., & Panigo, D. (2016). El impacto de la Política Automotriz Común (PAC) sobre la industria autopartista de Argentina y Brasil. *FES Argentina. Análisis*, 5. Retrieved December 02, 2024, from https://library.fes.de/pdf-files/bueros/argentinien/12529.pdf

Giannoni, W. (2022). Automotrices: cuántos operarios tiene hoy la industria en Córdoba. *La Voz del Interior*, 6 Junio 2022. Retrieved December 02, 2024, from https://www.lavoz.com.ar/politica/automotrices-cuantos-operarios-tiene-hoy-la-industria-en-cordoba

IFR. (2019). World robotics 2019. Industrial Robots. *International Federation of Robotics*. Retrieved December 02, 2024, from https://ifr.org/img/office/Sales_Flyer_World_Robotics_2019_web.pdf

ILO. (2020). The future of work in the automotive industry: The need to invest in people's capabilities and decent and sustainable work. *Issues paper for the Technical Meeting on the Future of Work in the Automotive Industry*. Geneva, 15–19 February 2021, International Labour Office, Sectoral Policies Department, Geneva, ILO, 2020. Retrieved December 02, 2024, from https://www.ilo.org/sites/default/files/wcmsp5/groups/public/%40ed_dialogue/%40sector/documents/meetingdocument/wcms_741659.pdf

INDEC. (2023). Complejos exportadores. *Comercio exterior. Vol. 8*, n° 4. *Informes técnicos. Vol. 8*, n° 46. Retrieved December 02, 2024, from https://www.indec.gob.ar/uploads/informesdeprensa/complejos_03_24B0330413F2.pdf

INDEC. (2024). Sistema de Cuentas Nacionales. Informe de avance en el nivel de actividad. 1° Trimestre de 2024. Retrieved December 02, 2024, from https://www.indec.gob.ar/uploads/informesdeprensa/pib_06_242C4E01A10F.pdf

Jürgens, U., & Krzywdzinski M. (2016). *New worlds of work. Varieties of work in car factories in the BRIC countries*. Oxford University Press. https://doi.org/10.1093/acprof:oso/9780198722670.001.0001

Keienburg, G. Gauger, Ch., Kengelbach, J., Degen, D., & Bruckner, P. (2019). As Tech transforms auto, deals are booming. Boston Consulting Group. Retrieved December 02, 2024, fromhttps://boston-consulting-group-brightspot.s3.amazonaws.com/img-src/BCG-As-Tech-Transforms-Auto-Deals-Are-Booming-August-2019_tcm9-227705.pdf

Krzywdzinski, M. (2021). Automation, digitalisation, and changes in occupational structures in the automobile industry in Germany, Japan, and the United States: A brief history from the early 1990s until 2018. *Industrial and Corporate Change, 30*(3), 499–535. https://doi.org/10.1093/icc/dtab019

Krzywdzinski, M. (2017). Automation, skill requirements and labour-use strategies: High-wage and low-wage approaches to high-tech manufacturing in the automotive industry. *New Technology, Work and Employment, 32*(3), 247–267. https://doi.org/10.1111/ntwe.12100

Lloyd, C., & Payne, J. (2023). Digital skills in context: Working with robots in lower-skilled jobs. *Economic and Industrial Democracy, 44*(4), 1084–1104. https://doi.org/10.1177/0143831X221111416

MECON. (2023). Misión 4. Impulsar la movilidad sustentable con productos y tecnologías nacionales. *Argentina Productiva 2030. Plan para el Desarrollo Productivo, Industrial y Tecnológico,* Documento de Trabajo No. 4. Retrieved December 02, 2024, from https://www.argentina.gob.ar/sites/default/files/mision_4_0.pdf

Montobbio, F., Staccioli, J., Virgillito, M. E., & Vivarelli, M. (2022). Robots and the origin of their labour-saving impact. *Technological Forecasting and Social Change, 174,* 121122. https://doi.org/10.1016/j.techfore.2021.121122

Nava, A. (2022). Negociación colectiva y cambio tecnológico en la Argentina: El caso de la industria automotriz y del sector petrolero. *Realidad Económica, 52*(349), 37-a. Retrieved December 02, 2024, from https://ojs.iade.org.ar/index.php/re/article/view/179/169

Pan, C. (2021). *Relaciones entre automatización avanzada y empleo: El caso de la industria autopartista en Argentina* (No. 805). Serie Documentos de Trabajo UCEMA. https://hdl.handle.net/10419/248619.

Raffaghelli, L. (2023). El impacto de las nuevas tecnologías informatizadas y los cambios en el empleo del sector automotriz. Empleo, desempleo and políticas de empleo. *CEIL-CONICET.* No. 27. Cuarto Trimestre 2023. Retrieved December 02, 2024, from http://repositorio.unm.edu.ar:8080/jspui/bitstream/123456789/737/1/PVT-DEYA-01-2022%20articulo%20neffa%203.pdf

Rajesh Kumar, B. (2012). Mergers and acquisitions in the automobile sector. In *Mega mergers and acquisitions* (pp. 210–214). Palgrave Macmillan. https://doi.org/10.1057/9781137005908_9

Riccio, F., Cresti, L., & Virgillito, M. E. (2024). The labour share along global value chains: Perspectives and evidence from sectoral interdependence. *Review of World Economics.* https://doi.org/10.1007/s10290-024-00555-3

OEDE. (2024). Estudios y estadísticas laborales. Observatorio de empleo y Dinámica Empresarial. Secretaría de empleo. Ministerio de Capital Humano.

Retrieved December 02, 2024, from https://www.argentina.gob.ar/trabajo/estadisticas/observatorio-de-empleo-y-dinamica-empresarial-oede-0.

Stöllinger, R. (2021). Testing the smile curve: Functional specialisation and value creation in GVCs. *Structural Change and Economic Dynamics, 56,* 93–116. https://doi.org/10.1016/j.strueco.2020.10.002

Wenten, F. (2017). Does it matter what workers do? The role of workers' relational agency in the hybridisation of TNC subsidiaries in China and Mexico. *International Journal of Automotive Technology and Management, 17*(2), 190–207. https://doi.org/10.1504/IJATM.2017.084803

Yin, R. (2014). *Case study research and applications design and methods.* Sage Publishers. Retrieved December 02, 2024, from https://uk.sagepub.com/en-gb/eur/case-study-research-and-applications/book250150

Index

A
Automated Guided Vehicles in the three companies, 49
A workplace analysis: case selection and fieldwork, 42

B
Background and theoretical framework: production, technology, and decisions in the periphery, 134
Barriers to adoption, 112
The boundaries of automation and digitalization on labour processes, 2

C
Case selection strategy: three different cases of AGVs adoption, 42
The company, the productive process and the local landscape of automotive production, 140
Concluding remarks and future challenges for social actors, 120

D
Digitalization and automation of healthcare technological solutions, 69
Digital technologies and changes in the Italian health care sector, 68
Drivers of adoption, 109

E
The execution of the fieldwork, 44

F
Findings, 109

Findings: digitalization and changes in organizational processes and working conditions of healthcare personnel, 79

I
Institutional challenges in healthcare digitization, 71
Interviews conducted at the plant level, 138
Interviews on State role dimensions, 139

L
Labor impact and the role of trade unions, 115
Labour process restructuring in relation to AGVs, 51
Logistics and Warehouses, 20

M
Methodology, 17, 77, 137
Methodology - a workplace analysis, 106

O
Overview of the main findings, 141

P
Productive reconversion, local context and technological change, 150
Putting AGVs in context, 39

R
Recent trends in the Italian healthcare labour market: wage compression and labour shortages, 72
Remote monitoring in healthcare, 23
The remote monitoring of implantable devices for patients with chronicity, 80
Results and main findings, 140
Results from qualitative analyses, 45
Robots in professional cleaning, 27

S
Selected Case Studies, 75
Setting the scene, 99
Summary of technologies and contexts of implementation, 79

T
Task reconfiguration in relation to AGVs, 55
The technological dimension, 102
Technological skills accumulation and shop floor culture, 145
Technologies and autonomy/dependence relationships of the local subsidiary, 143
Technologies of interest, 73
The technologies of interest, selected case studies, and methodology, 73
Technology and the transformation of the work process, 19
The telestroke technology system and Lifepak 15 for emergency treatment, 82
Time management as a key variable to understand techno-organizational

changes and their impact on working conditions, 86

V
Vulnerable Workers Under Automation and Digitalization, 7

W
Work activity: control and self-latitude of work, 50
Work organization: replacement/displacement dynamics, 48